SCOTT FORESMAN · ADDISON WESLEY

Mathematics

Grade 3

Spiral Review and Test Prep Masters

PEARSON

Scott Foresman

Editorial Offices: Glenview, Illinois • Parsippany, New Jersey • New York, New

Sales Offices: Parsippany, New Jersey • Duluth, Georgia • Glenview, Illinois
Coppell, Texas • Ontario, California • Mesa, Arizona

Overview

Spiral Review Test Prep provides students with a continuous review of concepts presented in earlier lessons or in the previous grade. There is a one-page *Spiral Review Test Prep* for each pupil lesson with questions in multiple-choice and free-response format.

ISBN 0-328-04979-4

2 3 4 5 6 7 8 9 10 V084 09 08 07 06 05 04 03

Spiral Review and Test Prep 1-1

Circle the correct answer.

1. Add.

$$\begin{array}{r} 16 \\ + 8 \\ \hline \end{array}$$

   A. 24
   B. 25
   C. 26
   D. 27

2. Subtract.

$$\begin{array}{r} 13 \\ - 7 \\ \hline \end{array}$$

   A. 7
   B. 6
   C. 5
   D. 4

3. Subtract.

$$\begin{array}{r} 16 \\ - 10 \\ \hline \end{array}$$

   A. 6
   B. 7
   C. 8
   D. 26

4. Which numbers continue the pattern?

2, 4, 6, 8, ___, ___, ___

   A. 9, 10, 11
   B. 12, 16, 24
   C. 14, 20, 26
   D. 10, 12, 14

5. Give the total amount of money pictured below.

_____

6. Write the fact family for 3, 5, and 8.

_____

_____

_____

7. The great white shark has 26 front-row teeth in the upper jaw and 24 in the lower jaw. How many more teeth are in the upper row?

_____

Spiral Review and Test Prep 1-2

Circle the correct answer.

1. Which numbers continue the pattern?

2, 6, 10, ___, ___, ___

A. 14, 18, 21
B. 13, 18, 20
C. 14, 18, 22
D. 13, 16, 19

2. Add.

```
   23
 +  7
```

A. 31
B. 30
C. 29
D. 28

3. Subtract.

```
   17
 −  8
```

A. 6
B. 7
C. 8
D. 9

4. Which would be the longest if measured?

A. a new pencil
B. a paper clip
C. a new crayon
D. a new piece of chalk

Use the picture to answer Exercises 5 and 6.

5. Which runner is first?

Finish Line

_____

6. Write the ordinal number for Runner C's place in the race.

_____

7. Write these numbers in order from greatest to least.

12   121   212   21   102

_____

_____

Spiral Review and Test Prep 1-3

Circle the correct answer.

1. How many ones are in the number 54?

   A. 9   **C.** 4
   B. 5   **D.** 1

2. Add.

   28
   + 7
   _____

   A. 1
   B. 16
   C. 25
   D. 35

3. Subtract.

   28
   − 8
   _____

   A. 7
   B. 19
   C. 20
   D. 36

4. If silent reading starts at 2:00 P.M. and ends at 2:15 P.M., how long was silent reading?

   A. 1 hr
   B. 25 min
   C. 20 min
   D. 15 min

5. Write the word form for 854.

_____

_____

6. Write 5 hundreds, 8 ones in standard form.

_____

7. Write $600 + 70 + 5$ in standard form.

_____

8. Name an object used to measure.

_____

Spiral Review and Test Prep 1-4

Circle the correct answer.

1. Which digit has the greatest place value in 2,307?

A. 7   **C.** 2
B. 3   **D.** 0

2. Subtract.

22 − 7

A. 13
B. 14
C. 15
D. 16

3. 342 can be renamed as

A. 3 hundreds, 42 ones.
B. 3 hundreds, 42 tens.
C. 1 hundred, 34 tens, 2 ones.
D. 1 hundred, 24 tens, 42 ones.

4. Add.

53 + 8

A. 60
B. 61
C. 62
D. 63

5. Write the number in standard form.

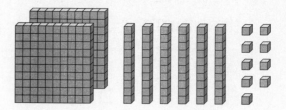

_____

6. What time is shown on the clock?

_____

7. Stephanie had 22 marbles. She gave Maggie and Sylvia each 4 marbles. How many marbles does Stephanie have left?

_____

Name_____

Spiral Review and Test Prep 1-5

● Circle the correct answer.

1. How would you write this number in standard form? Seven thousand, two hundred thirty-seven

   A. 7,737   **C.** 7,273
   B. 7,372   **D.** 7,237

2. Subtract.   **A.** 10
                 B. 11
   16   **C.** 12
   − 5   **D.** 13

3. Name these 3 shapes.

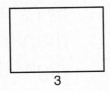

   1   2   3

   A.
   1: triangle
   2: square
   3: cylinder

   C.
   1: triangle
   2: rectangle
   3: square

   B.
   1: triangle
   2: rectangle
   3: sphere

   D.
   1: triangle
   2: square
   3: rectangle

4. Write 16 tens and 4 ones in standard form.

   _____

5. Write 3,024 in expanded form.

   _____

   _____

6. Draw the next picture in the pattern.

Spiral Review and Test Prep 1-6

Circle the correct answer. Use the table to answer Exercises 1 and 2.

Animals Seen on Hike

Kind	Number
Deer	II
Bird	IIIII II
Squirrel	IIIII
Rabbit	III

1. How many deer did they see?

   A. 2   **C.** 5

   B. 3   **D.** 7

2. Which animal did they see most often?

   A. Deer   **C.** Squirrel

   B. Bird   **D.** Rabbit

3. How would you write this number in standard form? five hundred twenty thousand, two hundred three

   A. 502,203 **C.** 520,203

   B. 502,230 **D.** 520,230

4. What place is the 9 in the number 410,928?

_____

5. José found money in the sand at the beach. He found 2 quarters, 1 dime, 4 nickels, and 2 pennies. What was the total amount of money he found?

_____

6. Write the number whose thousands digit is 7, tens digit is 2 more than the thousands digit, the hundreds digit is 6 less than the tens digit, and the ones digit is 3 more than the hundreds digit.

_____

Spiral Review and Test Prep 1-7

Circle the correct answer.

1. What is the word form of 604?

A. sixty-four
B. six hundred four
C. six hundred forty
D. sixty-four hundred

2. Subtract.

$$\begin{array}{r} 25 \\ -\ 16 \\ \hline \end{array}$$

A. 8
B. 9
C. 11
D. 14

3. Which picture is an example of a flip?

A.

B.

C.

D.

Write each number in standard form.

4. fifty-eight thousand, one hundred sixty

_____

5. 300,000 + 50,000 + 2,000 + 100 + 80 + 4

_____

A family ordered 1 large pizza and 2 medium pizzas for dinner. The medium pizzas were cut into 6 slices each and the large was cut into 8 slices. How many slices of pizza are there in all?

6. Solve the problem and write your answer in a complete sentence.

_____

_____

_____

Spiral Review and Test Prep 1-8

Circle the correct answer.

1. How would you write this number in standard form? Two hundred thousand, six hundred ninety-nine

    A. 200,699
    B. 206,990
    C. 209,699
    D. 269,600

2. Which is equal to 62 tens?

    A. 6   **C.** 620
    B. 62   **D.** 6,200

3. Darren has 500 baseball cards and 203 football cards. How many cards does he have in all?

    A. 753
    B. 730
    C. 723
    D. 703

Use the table for 4–6. For each exercise, compare the heights of the two trees. Use <, >, or =.

National Champion Trees

Tree Type	Height (in ft)
Giant sequoia	275
Sugar pine	232
Coast Douglas fir	281
Port Orford cedar	219
Coast redwood	321

4. Giant sequoia ◯ Coast redwood

5. Sugar pine ◯ Port Orford cedar

6. Coast Douglas fir ◯ Coast redwood

Spiral Review and Test Prep 1-9

● Circle the correct answer.

1. How would you write this number in standard form?

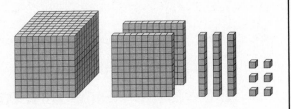

A. 1,236   **C.** 2,136
B. 1,326   **D.** 2,236

2. Which is the order of 4,392; 3,999; 4,401 from greatest to least?

A. 3,999 4,392 4,401
B. 3,999 4,401 4,392
C. 4,392 4,401 3,999
D. 4,401 4,392 3,999

● **3.** Which would you use to measure the height of a giraffe?

A. inches
B. feet
C. miles
D. gallons

4. Fill in 1,655; 1,100; and 1,350 where they should be on the number line.

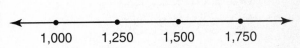

5. Candace had 22 stickers in her collection. She received 7 new stickers. How many stickers does Candace have in all?

_____

6. Which number is greater, 48,325 or 48,235?

_____

7. Write the numbers from least to greatest. 976, 987, 998, 974

_____

Spiral Review and Test Prep 1-10

Circle the correct answer.

1. Continue the pattern.

36, 30, 24, ___, ___, ___

A. 14, 10, 8
B. 18, 12, 6
C. 28, 22, 26
D. 38, 32, 36

2. 24 books − ___ books = 17 books

A. 7   **C.** 5
B. 6   **D.** 4

3. Which object weighs about 1 kilogram?

A. a crayon
B. a car
C. a book
D. a computer

4. What is the word form of 725?

A. seven hundred
B. seven hundred fifty
C. seven hundred twenty-five
D. seven hundred five

5. Write 3,549 in expanded form.

_____

_____

6. Don had 3 toy cars. Each week his allowance helps him to buy 2 more cars. If he buys cars for 5 weeks, how many toy cars will he have total by the fifth week?

_____

Write the numbers in order from least to greatest.

7. 454, 450, 545, 451

_____

8. 4,396; 3,996; 4,369; 3,946

_____

Spiral Review and Test Prep 1-11

● Circle the correct answer.

1. Which number is greater than 235,187?

    A. 225,187
    B. 234,988
    C. 235,167
    D. 235,188

2. Which number continues the pattern?
23, 19, 15, ——, ——, ——

    A. 11, 7, 3   **C.** 12, 8, 4
    B. 11, 7, 4   **D.** 12, 9, 5

3. When the Clarks first bought a door for their closet, it was 84 in. long. It had to be cut down 12 in. to fit into the opening already there. How long was the opening for the door?

    A. 70 in.   **C.** 74 in.
    B. 72 in.   **D.** 76 in.

Round to the nearest ten.

4. 88 _____

5. 421 _____

Round to the nearest hundred.

6. 736 _____

7. 574 _____

8. Use the chart below to list the lengths of the rivers from least to greatest.

North American Rivers

River	Length (in mi)
Peace River	1,210
Snake River	1,038
Mackenzie River	1,060
Columbia River	1,243

_____

_____

_____

_____

Spiral Review and Test Prep 1-12

Circle the correct answer.

1. Round 5,456 to the nearest hundred.

   A. 5,400   C. 5,500
   B. 5,450   D. 5,550

2. Add.

   $590 + 110$

   A. 600
   B. 610
   C. 700
   D. 730

3. Choose the correct operations to make this equation true:

   13 ___ 7 ___ 3 = 17.

   A. −, +   C. −, −
   B. +, +   D. +, −

4. In a bag are 3 red, 1 blue, and 4 green blocks. Which color is most likely to be picked from the bag?

   A. Blue   C. Green
   B. Red   D. Yellow

James traveled to Kentucky, New York, California, and Illinois. Tom traveled to Illinois, Florida, North Carolina, and New York. Which states were visited by both boys? Here is Mary's approach to solving the problem.

James	Tom
Kentucky	Florida
New York	New York
California	North Carolina
Illinois	Illinois

5. Which strategy was used to solve the problem?

   _____

6. Use the problem in Exercise 5. Write the answer in a complete sentence.

   _____

   _____

Spiral Review and Test Prep 1-13

Circle the correct answer.

1. Add.

$$\begin{array}{r} 58¢ \\ +\ 24¢ \\ \hline \end{array}$$

A. 72¢   **C.** 86¢

B. 82¢   **D.** 96¢

2. Finish the pattern.

14, 17, 20, 23, ___, ___,

___

A. 26, 29, 33

B. 25, 28, 30

C. 26, 29, 32

D. 25, 27, 29

3. How would you write this number in standard form?

A. 4,002   **C.** 420

B. 4,000   **D.** 42

4. Tell what coins you could use to show $0.28 in two ways.

_____

_____

_____

_____

_____

5. Louis found 4 coins on the ground. The total value was $0.46. What coins did he find?

_____

_____

_____

_____

Spiral Review and Test Prep 1-14

Circle the correct answer.

1. Peter had a $5 bill. He purchased a baseball for $2.99. How much change did he receive?

- **A.** $7.99
- **C.** $2.01
- **B.** $3.01
- **D.** $1.99

2. How much money is shown?

- **A.** $6.57
- **C.** $6.72
- **B.** $6.67
- **D.** $6.77

3. What is the value of the 5 in this number?

405,729

- **A.** 5 × 10
- **B.** 5 × 100
- **C.** 5 × 1,000
- **D.** 5 × 10,000

Compare. Use <, >, or =.

4. 3,686 _____ 3,686

5. 51,231 _____ 52,530

6. Write the numbers from greatest to least.

961, 971, 917, 916, 977

_____

7. Phil has 10 golf balls. His friend Steve has twice as many as Phil. Their friend Paul has 2 more than Phil and Steve together. How many does Steve have?

_____

How many golf balls does Paul have?

_____

How many do Steve and Paul have altogether?

_____

Name_____

Spiral Review and Test Prep 1-15

Circle the correct answer.

1. What is 67,452 rounded to the nearest hundred?

A. 67,400 **C.** 67,450
B. 67,500 **D.** 67,550

2. What ordinal number would come next in the following list?

94th, 95th, 96th, _____

A. 99th **C.** 97th
B. 98th **D.** 93rd

3. What is the name of the following solid figure?

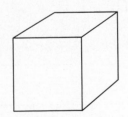

A. Cylinder
B. Cube
C. Pyramid
D. Sphere

Each football team has 3 coaches. There are 7 teams in the league. How many coaches are there? Look back and check Andy's work on this problem.

Andy's Work

Team	Coaches
1	3
2	3
3	3
4	3
5	3
6	3

There are 18 coaches.

4. Did he answer the right question?

_____

5. Is his work correct?

_____

_____

_____

Spiral Review and Test Prep 2-1

Circle the correct answer.

1. Add.

$$\begin{array}{r} 12 \\ +\ \ 4 \\ \hline \end{array}$$

A. 14
B. 16
C. 18
D. 20

2. Subtract.

$$\begin{array}{r} 30 \\ -\ 10 \\ \hline \end{array}$$

A. 10
B. 15
C. 20
D. 25

3. If Maritza buys a liter of pop that costs $1.19 with $2.00, which would be her change?

   A. 1 penny, 3 quarters
   B. 1 penny, 1 nickel, 3 quarters
   C. 1 penny, 1 dime, 3 quarters
   D. 1 nickel, 3 quarters

4. Which is the value of the 4 in the number 24,302?

   A. 4   C. 400
   B. 40   D. 4,000

Compare the numbers. Use <, >, or =.

5. 673 ___ 773

6. 2,107 ___ 2,017

Carlie is paid $5.00 a day for babysitting. If she babysits for 5 days, how much will Carlie earn?

Ray's Work

Day	1	2	3	4	5
Money Earned	$5	$10	$15	$20	$25

Carlie will earn $25 after 5 days.

7. Is Ray's work correct? Explain.

_____

_____

_____

_____

Spiral Review and Test Prep 2-2

Circle the correct answer. | Write each missing number.

1. Which number would be the farthest to the right on a number line?

A. 672   **C.** 978
B. 872   **D.** 982

2. Which property is shown below?

$7 + 4 + 2 = 2 + 4 + 7$

A. Zero Property of Addition
B. Associative Property of Addition
C. Identity Property of Addition
D. Commutative Property of Addition

3. Add.

$4 + 19 =$

A. 20   **C.** 22
B. 21   **D.** 23

4. $15 = $ _____ $ + (4 + 4)$

5. $9 + $ _____ $ = 9$

6. $7 + 8 = $ _____ $ + 7$

7. Write the word name for 803.

_____

_____

8. Wanda collected cans for recycling. She collected 4 cans on Monday, 3 cans on Tuesday, 6 cans on Wednesday, 5 cans on Thursday, and 4 cans on Friday. How many total cans did Wanda collect altogether?

_____

Spiral Review and Test Prep 2-3

Circle the correct answer.

1. Round to the nearest ten.

568

A. 56   **C.** 560
B. 57   **D.** 570

2. Which number is less than 751?

A. 792   **C.** 749
B. 751   **D.** 789

3. How would you write the number 845,212 in expanded form?

A. 800,000 + 4,000 + 5,000 + 200 + 12
B. 800,000 + 40,000 + 500 + 200 + 12
C. 800,000 + 40,000 + 5,000 + 200 + 10 + 2
D. 80,000 + 40,000 + 500 + 200 + 1 + 2

Complete the fact family.

4. 6 + 7 = _____

13 − _____ = 7

_____ + 6 = 13

_____ − 7 = 6

Josephine has 12 bracelets. She gives 4 bracelets to her friend Monica. How many bracelets does she have left?

5. What strategy could you use to solve this problem?

_____

_____

6. Solve the problem. Write the answer in a complete sentence.

_____

_____

© Pearson Education, Inc. 3

Spiral Review and Test Prep 2-4

Circle the correct answer.

1. How would you write this number in standard form?

6 hundreds, 3 tens, 2 ones

A. 632   **C.** 362

B. 623   **D.** 236

2. Which is the rule for the table?

In	9	5	7	13	12	6
Out	7	3	5	11		

A. Add 2
B. Subtract 3
C. Add 3
D. Subtract 2

3. Round to the nearest hundred.

1,233

A. 1,300   **C.** 1,200

B. 1,250   **D.** 1,000

4. Jamel has 5 quarters, 2 dimes, 1 nickel, and 2 pennies. How much money does he have altogether?

_____

5. Complete the pattern.

2, 4, 7, 9, 12, 14, _____,

_____, _____

6. Samuel leaves for work at 8:00 A.M. to arrive at work by 9:00 A.M. He stays at work for 8 hr. If it takes him the same amount of time to get home as it did to arrive at work, what time will Samuel get home from work?

_____

_____

Spiral Review and Test Prep 2-5

Circle the correct answer.

1. $7 + 3 = 3 +$ _____

   A. 4   **C.** 6

   B. 5   **D.** 7

2. Which ordinal number would come next?

33rd, 34th, 35th,

   A. 38th   **C.** 36th

   B. 37th   **D.** 34th

3. Which number sentence would you write to solve the following problem?

Kelly bought 4 apples and 3 oranges. How many pieces of fruit did Kelly buy?

   A. $4 - 3 = n$

   B. $3 - 4 = n$

   C. $4 + 3 = n$

   D. $4 - n = 3$

Space Program In 1959, 7 test pilots were chosen as the first group of pilot astronauts. NASA selected 9 more in 1962. In 1963, NASA added twice as many astronauts as in 1959. How many pilot astronauts were selected in 1963?

Joe's Work

1959	7	astronauts
1962	9	astronauts
	16	astronauts

There were 16 astronauts in 1962.

4. Did Joe answer the right question? Explain.

_____

_____

_____

5. What is the solution to the problem?

_____

_____

_____

Name_____

Spiral Review and Test Prep 2-6

Circle the correct answer.

1. Which is the number in standard form?

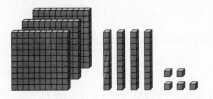

A. 534   **C.** 345
B. 435   **D.** 343

2. To add 27 + 32 Tom first thought to add 20 + 30 = 50. Which two numbers should Tom add next?

A. 0 + 2   **C.** 7 + 2
B. 3 + 2   **D.** 3 + 0

3. Which three numbers come next in the pattern?

4, 7, 5, 8, 6, 9, 7, ____, ____, ____

A. 10, 8, 11
B. 9, 12, 10
C. 10, 13, 11
D. 9, 7, 10

Rocket	Height
Mercury-Redstone	83 ft
A Class Soviet	98 ft
Saturn V	363 ft

If these rockets were placed on top of each other, how tall would they be?

4. Tell what the question is asking.

_____

_____

_____

_____

5. Solve the problem. Write the answer in a complete sentence.

_____

_____

_____

Spiral Review and Test Prep 2-7

Circle the correct answer.

1. The number on Dave's house is 612. What is this number used for?

   A. to locate
   B. to measure
   C. to count
   D. to name

2. Which of the following shows 842 in expanded form?

   A. $800 + 40 + 20$
   B. $80 + 400 + 2$
   C. $800 + 40 + 2$
   D. $80 + 40 + 2$

3. Theresa has 6 dimes, 4 quarters, and a $5 bill. How much money does she have?

   A. $5.85   C. $6.60
   B. $6.25   D. $6.85

Find each sum using mental math.

4. $77 + 5 =$ _____

5. $64 + 12 =$ _____

6. $18 + 25 =$ _____

Solve the problem. Look back and check your work.

7. Flavio earned $35.00 last week for cutting lawns. This week he has earned $10.00 on Monday, $10.00 on Tuesday, $5.00 on Wednesday, and $5.00 on Thursday. How much money does Flavio need to earn on Friday so that he earns the same amount of money as last week?

   _____

   _____

© Pearson Education, Inc. 3

Spiral Review and Test Prep 2-8

● Circle the correct answer.

1. Add.

    25
+ 33

A. 52
B. 55
C. 58
D. 60

2. Grace had 12 pens. She bought 5 more, then gave away 7. How many pens does she have now?

A. 5   **C.** 10
B. 7   **D.** 12

3. Find the sum.

$(0 + 7) + (2 + 3) =$

A. 10   **C.** 13
B. 12   **D.** 15

4. How would you write seven hundred forty-nine in standard form?

A. 704   **C.** 749
B. 744   **D.** 794

5. Use compatible numbers to estimate the sum of 246 + 123.

_____

6. Write the numbers in order from least to greatest.

2,234 3,402 2,564
3,681 22,243

_____

_____

_____

7. There are 20 students and 5 adults going on a field trip. If there is 1 adult for each group and there are the same amount of students in each group, how many students will be in each group?

_____

Spiral Review and Test Prep 2-9

Circle the correct answer.

1. Find the missing number.

$4 + (3 + 9) = $ _____ $+ (9 + 4)$

A. 3   **C.** 12

B. 5   **D.** 13

2. Which number would be farthest to the left on a number line?

A. 10   **C.** 14

B. 12   **D.** 16

3. Which of the following is an underestimate for 286 + 158?

A. 300   **C.** 450

B. 400   **D.** 500

4. What is the name of this shape?

A. square
B. rectangle
C. pentagon
D. hexagon

5. Write two thousand, three hundred nine in standard form.

_____

Mountain climbers planned to climb a 6,926 ft mountain. If the hikers hike 500 ft each day, about how many days will it take them to climb to the top of the mountain?

6. Steve says it will take the hikers 15 days. Is Steve correct? Explain.

_____

_____

_____

_____

7. Solve the problem. Write the answer in a complete sentence.

_____

_____

Name_____

Spiral Review and Test Prep 2-10

Circle the correct answer.

1. Pamela bought $7.89 worth of cheese. She paid with a $10 bill. How much change did she receive?

   A. $3.21   C. $2.11
   B. $2.21   D. $1.21

2. Which combination of coins could you use to show $1.21?

   A. one $1 bill, one dime
   B. four quarters, one dime, one penny
   C. one $1 bill, two dimes, one penny
   D. four quarters, four nickels

3. Lorraine is 5th in line. Channel is after her in line. Which place is Channel in line?

   A. 5th   C. 7th
   B. 6th   D. 8th

Find each difference using mental math.

4. 61 − 9 = _____

5. 89 − 18 = _____

6. 94 − 27 = _____

Joe can pack 4 pillows into each box. How many boxes will he need if the family has a total of 12 pillows?

Kerry's Solution

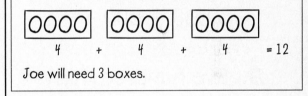

4 + 4 + 4 = 12

Joe will need 3 boxes.

7. What strategy did Kerry use to solve the problem?

_____

8. What is another strategy you could use to solve this problem?

_____

Spiral Review and Test Prep 2-11

Circle the correct answer.

1. What number comes next in the pattern?

18, 22, 26, _____

A. 24   **C.** 30
B. 28   **D.** 34

2. Which number is greater than 234,592?

A. 234,601
B. 233,999
C. 200,000 + 30,000 + 3,000 + 500 + 80 + 3
D. two hundred thirty-three thousand

3. If 3 people are in front of Jeremy in line, what place in line is he?

A. first   **C.** third
B. second **D.** fourth

4. Count on to find the difference mentally.

$67 - 28 =$ _____

During the basketball tournament, Kiki scored 27 points, Tanya scored 11 points, Sung Lee scored 22, and Penelope scored 8. How many points did they score altogether?

5. Tell the problem in your own words.

_____

_____

_____

_____

6. Solve the problem. Write the answer in a complete sentence.

_____

_____

Spiral Review and Test Prep 2-12

Circle the correct answer.

1. Round 888 to the nearest hundred.

    A. 800   **C.** 900

    B. 880   **D.** 980

2. Which of the following is the same as 6 hundreds, 13 ones?

    A. 613   **C.** 713

    B. 630   **D.** 730

3. Which sentence is true?

    A. $345 < 336$

    B. $290 > 309$

    C. $129 = 127 + 3$

    D. $455 > 425 + 20$

4. Round to the nearest ten to estimate the difference for $346 - 252$.

    A. 110   **C.** 90

    B. 100   **D.** 80

5. Evaluate the expression if $x = 5$.

$(13 + x) + 7 =$ _____

Janey, Nikita, and Tyler want to combine their money to buy a computer game that costs $49.78. Janey has $15.00, Nikita has $15.00, and Tyler has $20.00. Do they have enough money to buy the game?

6. Show the main idea.

_____

7. Solve the problem. Write your answer in a complete sentence.

_____

_____

_____

_____

Spiral Review and Test Prep 2-13

Circle the correct answer.

1. Round to the nearest hundred and estimate the sum.

768 + 119

A. 800   **C.** 900

B. 890   **D.** 950

2. Which number comes next in this pattern?

100, 150, 200, 250, 300, _____

A. 350   **C.** 450

B. 400   **D.** 500

3. Jane counted the loose change in her purse. How much money did she have altogether?

A. $1.28   **C.** $1.53

B. $1.48   **D.** $1.63

4. Write the following numbers in order from least to greatest.

367, 376, 366, 377, 306, 307

_____

_____

Stan has 643 baseball cards. Lou has 869 baseball cards. About how many more cards does Lou have than Stan?

5. Is an exact answer or an estimate needed for this problem? Explain.

_____

_____

_____

_____

6. Solve the problem.

_____

Spiral Review and Test Prep 3-1

Circle the correct answer.

1. Which ordinal number comes next?

42nd, 43rd, 44th, _____

A. 43rd   **C.** 54th
B. 45th   **D.** 56th

2. Find the missing number.

$0 +$ _____ $= 7$

A. 7   **C.** 5
B. 6   **D.** 0

3. What time is shown on the clock?

A. 3:15   **C.** 4:16
B. 3:20   **D.** 4:20

Write a number sentence. Then solve the problem.

4. President Rutherford B. Hayes was the father of 8 children. President John Tyler had 14 children. How many more children did President Tyler have than President Hayes?

_____

_____

Complete each fact family.

5. $5 + 7 =$ ___

___ $- 5 = 7$

___ $+ 5 = 12$

___ $- 7 = 5$

6. $8 + 6 =$ ___

___ $- 8 = 6$

___ $+ 8 = 14$

___ $- 6 = 8$

Spiral Review and Test Prep 3-2

Circle the correct answer.

1. Estimate the sum by rounding to the nearest hundred.

   $104 + 287$

   A. 200   **C.** 400
   B. 300   **D.** 500

2. Find the sum using mental math.

   $37 + 29$

   A. 57   **C.** 66
   B. 59   **D.** 67

3. Which of the following is equal to $(5 + 1) + 7$?

   A. $(5 + 8) + 2$
   B. $(7 + 2) + 5$
   C. $5 + (1 + 7)$
   D. $7 + (5 + 7)$

Add.

4. $\begin{array}{r} 27 \\ + \ 31 \\ \hline \end{array}$

5. $\begin{array}{r} 58 \\ + \ 17 \\ \hline \end{array}$

6. The planet Uranus has 11 rings. Neptune has 4 rings. How many rings do they have altogether?

   Write a number sentence and solve the problem.

   _____

Complete the pattern.

7. 39, 36, 33, ____, ____,

   ____

Spiral Review and Test Prep 3-3

Circle the correct answer.

1. The rule for Brandy's table is Subtract 3. What should she put in to get out 7?

A. 4   **C.** 10
B. 7   **D.** 13

2. How would you write this number in standard form?

two thousand, four hundred, twenty-three

A. 20,423   **C.** 2,423
B. 2,432   **D.** 2,403

3. Subtract.

11 − 6

A. 2   **C.** 4
B. 3   **D.** 5

4. Which number is the greatest?

A. 624   **C.** 426
B. 462   **D.** 642

5. Write the fact family for 2, 7, and 9.

_____

_____

Write the problem and find the sum.

6.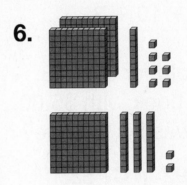

_____

7. Stan's family drove 159 mi on Monday and 224 mi on Tuesday. How many miles did they drive? Solve the problem. Explain how you got your answer.

_____

_____

Spiral Review and Test Prep 3-4

Circle the correct answer.

1. Which shows adding 35 + 13 by breaking apart numbers?

   A. 35 + 13
   B. 35 + 10 + 30
   C. 35 + 31
   D. 35 + 10 + 3

2. Alex paid for a $2.98 comic book with $5.00. What was his change?

   A. $3.92   C. $2.12
   B. $3.02   D. $2.02

3. Round 75 to the nearest ten.

   A. 70   C. 77
   B. 75   D. 80

At the school fair, each game costs 3 tickets. Miriam tried to figure out how many games she could play with 18 tickets.

Miriam's Work

Tickets	Games
3	1
6	2
9	3
11	4
13	5
15	6
17	7

seven games and one ticket left over

4. Is Miriam's work correct? Explain.

   _____

   _____

   _____

   _____

   _____

5. Round to the nearest hundred to estimate

   729 + 168. _____

© Pearson Education, Inc. 3

Name_____

Spiral Review and Test Prep 3-5

Circle the correct answer.

1. Estimate the sum by rounding. Which of the following would be an underestimate?

178 + 21

A. 180   **C.** 200
B. 199   **D.** 201

2. How many tens are in 270?

A. 2   **C.** 17
B. 7   **D.** 27

3. Which number makes this number sentence true?

0 + _____ = 12

A. 12   **C.** 1
B. 3   **D.** 0

4. Which number is the least?

A. 6,999   **C.** 6,991
B. 6,994   **D.** 6,990

5. Add.

```
   402
   329
   148
+  261
_____
```

Arkansas has 75 counties. Illinois has 102 counties. About how many more counties does Illinois have than Arkansas?

6. Is an exact answer or an estimate needed? Explain.

_____

_____

_____

_____

7. Solve the problem.

_____

_____

Spiral Review and Test Prep 3-6

Circle the correct answer.

1. How would you write 783 in expanded form?

   A. $700 + 800 + 30$

   B. $7 + 80 + 3$

   C. $700 + 80 + 3$

   D. $780 + 3$

2. Round to the nearest hundred to estimate the difference.

   $486 - 108$

   A. 300   **C.** 380

   B. 350   **D.** 400

3. There are 6 people ahead of Morito in line. Which place in line is Morito?

   A. fifth   **C.** seventh

   B. sixth   **D.** eighth

Use mental math.

4. $84 - 19 = $ _____

5. $136 - 21 = $ _____

Sampson made a snack for himself and 3 friends. Each person received 4 strawberries. How many strawberries did Sampson start with?

6. Draw a picture to solve the problem.

7. Explain how your drawing from Exercise 6 helped you solve the problem.

_____

_____

_____

Spiral Review and Test Prep 3-7

Circle the correct answer. | Regroup 1 ten for 10 ones.

1. What is the value of the underlined digit in 27,4<u>6</u>3?

A. 4   **C.** 400
B. 40   **D.** 4,000

2. There are 61 species of monkeys in Asia and Africa. South and Central America have 69 species of monkeys. About how many species of monkeys are there altogether in these places?

A. 100   **C.** 130
B. 120   **D.** 140

3. Henry has 2 hundreds, 4 tens, and 3 ones. How many tens will he have if he regroups a hundred?

A. 3   **C.** 13
B. 4   **D.** 14

4. ☐ ☐
84 = 8 tens 4 ones

5. ☐☐
58 = 5 tens 8 ones

6. ☐☐
32 = 3 tens 2 ones

7. The rule in Vivian's table is Subtract 5. What number will she get out if she puts in 27?

_____

8. Andy did 43 sit-ups. Harley did 57 sit-ups. How many more sit-ups did Harley do than Andy? Write a number sentence to solve the problem.

_____

_____

© Pearson Education, Inc. 3

Spiral Review and Test Prep 3-8

Circle the correct answer.

1. Which number is the sum of 14 and 21?

A. 7   **C.** 21
B. 14   **D.** 35

2. Bus 312 goes to the city. What do we use the number on the bus for?

A. to measure
B. to locate
C. to name
D. to count

3. Round to the nearest ten to estimate the difference.

185 − 102

A. 90   **C.** 150
B. 100   **D.** 200

4. Which number is greater than 562?

A. 572   **C.** 527
B. 560   **D.** 507

Subtract.

5.
$$\begin{array}{r} 59 \\ -\ 23 \\ \hline \end{array}$$

6.
$$\begin{array}{r} 88 \\ -\ 37 \\ \hline \end{array}$$

7. If you spent $4.68 at the movies, how much change would you receive from a $5 bill?

_____

8. Geraldine bought 4 blue bookmarks, 3 green bookmarks, and 6 erasers. How many bookmarks did she buy? Write a number sentence.

_____

_____

Spiral Review and Test Prep 3-9

Circle the correct answer.

1. Add.

$$\begin{array}{r} 149 \\ +26 \\ \hline \end{array}$$

A. 175
B. 174
C. 165
D. 164

2. Jason has 1 quarter, 4 dimes, 2 nickels, and 6 pennies. How much money does Jason have?

A. $0.71 **C.** $0.84
B. $0.81 **D.** $0.89

3. Which of the following is an overestimate for $478 + 367$?

A. 700 **C.** 800
B. 750 **D.** 1,000

4. Which of the following is FALSE?

A. $136 = 130 + 6$
B. $362 > 326$
C. $41 + 32 = 32 + 41$
D. $72 + 49 = 72 - 49$

Find each difference. You may draw place-value blocks to help.

5.
$$\begin{array}{r} 326 \\ -137 \\ \hline \end{array}$$

6.
$$\begin{array}{r} 274 \\ -106 \\ \hline \end{array}$$

7. Hal has $42. He buys a hat for $17. How much money does he have left? Write a number sentence to solve this problem.

_____

_____

8. Subtract.

$$\begin{array}{r} 47 \\ -28 \\ \hline \end{array}$$

Spiral Review and Test Prep 3-10

Circle the correct answer.

1. What is the name of this shape?

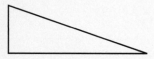

   A. Rectangle
   B. Triangle
   C. Square
   D. Diamond

2. Which number sentence completes the fact family?

$18 + 7 = 25$, $7 + 18 = 25$, $25 - 7 = 18$, _____

   A. $18 - 7 = 11$
   B. $25 - 18 = 7$
   C. $25 + 7 = 32$
   D. $7 + 25 = 32$

3. Add.

$$\begin{array}{r} 673 \\ + \ 112 \\ \hline \end{array}$$

   A. 765
   B. 785
   C. 865
   D. 875

4. Write $40{,}000 + 7{,}000 + 90 + 6$ in standard form.

_____

Subtract.

5.
$$\begin{array}{r} 946 \\ - \ 168 \\ \hline \end{array}$$

6.
$$\begin{array}{r} 381 \\ - \ 216 \\ \hline \end{array}$$

7. Crystal checks out 3 books each week at the library. How many books will she check out in 7 weeks? Explain how you solved the problem.

_____

_____

_____

_____

Spiral Review and Test Prep 3-11

Circle the correct answer.

1. Regroup 1 ten for 10 ones.

65

A. 6 tens, 5 ones
B. 6 tens, 10 ones
C. 5 tens, 10 ones
D. 5 tens, 15 ones

2. Add.

$13 + 7 + 12$

A. 32   **C.** 23
B. 30   **D.** 22

3. About how long would it take to tie your shoe?

A. 1 min   **C.** 1 day
B. 1 hr   **D.** 1 week

4. Round 417,394 to the nearest hundred.

A. 410,400 **C.** 418,000
B. 417,400 **D.** 427,000

Subtract.

5.   703
        − 123

6.   600
        − 327

Edith has 1 quarter, 3 dimes, 5 nickels, and 2 pennies. How much money does Edith have?

7. Is an exact answer or an estimate needed for this problem?

_____

8. What is the answer?

_____

9. Use $<$, $>$, or $=$.

3,417 _____ 3,502

Spiral Review and Test Prep 3-12

Circle the correct answer.

1. 6,000 + 500 + 30 + 2

    A. 650,000
    B. 65,302
    C. 6,532
    D. 6,523

2. Which is the missing number?

$$(6 + 9) + 4 = 4 + \_\_\_\_$$

    A. 4   **C.** 9
    B. 6   **D.** 15

3. Add.

    604
  + 281

    A. 885
    B. 883
    C. 875
    D. 863

4. Which number is next in this pattern?

44, 55, 66, _____

    A. 22   **C.** 77
    B. 33   **D.** 88

5. Write the numbers from least to greatest.

797   977   779

_____

Mr. Nation's class needs 200 points to earn a class party. They earned 62 points in January, 47 points in February, and 57 points in March. About how many more points do they need to earn their party?

6. What operation will you use to solve the problem?

_____

7. Write a number sentence to help solve the problem.

_____

_____

Spiral Review and Test Prep 3-13

● Circle the correct answer.

1. Anna rounded 4,738 to 4,740. What place did she round to?

   A. Ones
   B. Tens
   C. Hundreds
   D. Thousands

2. Use mental math to add.

   $176 + 312$

   A. 488   C. 484
   B. 486   D. 482

3. Use mental math to subtract.

   $419 - 212$

   A. 227   C. 207
   B. 217   D. 200

4. Which number makes this sentence true?

   $n + 7 = 17$

   A. 5   C. 8
   B. 7   D. 10

5. Write a number that has a 3 in the hundreds place.

   _____

6. Austin washed cars for the community fund-raiser. He earned $47.55 on Friday and $62.80 on Saturday. Write a number sentence that tells how much Austin earned.

   _____

   _____

Menu	
Salad	$1.85
Chicken sandwich	$1.99
Tuna salad	$3.27
Apple	$0.97
Milk	$0.74

7. How much more does a tuna salad cost than a chicken sandwich?

   _____

© Pearson Education, Inc. 3

Spiral Review and Test Prep 3-14

Circle the correct answer.

1. Which of the following is the rule?

In	7	8	9	10	11
Out	29	30	31	32	33

A. Add 19   **C.** Add 22
B. Add 20   **D.** Add 23

2. Which shows 30,000 + 7,000 + 9 in standard form?

A. 379   **C.** 30,709
B. 3,709   **D.** 37,009

3. There are 27 people ahead of Carrie in line. What is Carrie's place in line?

A. 27th   **C.** 29th
B. 28th   **D.** 30th

4. Round 504 to the nearest ten.

A. 500   **C.** 510
B. 504   **D.** 540

5. Estimate the sum of 732 + 122 using front-end estimation.

_____

Use mental math, paper and pencil, or a calculator to solve.

6.   29,472
      + 16,843
      _____

The deepest spot in the Pacific Ocean has a depth of 35,400 ft. The deepest spot in the Atlantic Ocean is 30,246 ft deep. What is the difference in the depths of the two oceans?

7. Write a number sentence to help to solve the problem. Then solve the problem.

_____

_____

Spiral Review and Test Prep 3-15

● Circle the correct answer.

1. April's rule is Add 9. She got out 17. What did she put in?

A. 4   C. 11
B. 8   D. 18

2. Add.

633
620
+ 71

A. 1,263
B. 1,324
C. 1,345
D. 1,353

● **3.** 2 quarters, 2 dimes, 2 nickels, and 2 pennies = _____

A. $0.22   C. $0.82
B. $0.28   D. $2.08

4. Which number sentence is true?

A. $12 + 5 > 19$
B. $18 + 9 = 7 + 20$
C. $42 < 20 + 20$
D. $11 + 1 = 11 - 1$

Long Jump

Brady	51 in.
Fiona	45 in.
Gwen	61 in.
Leon	49 in.
Randy	44 in.

5. Five students participated in the long jump. Write the students' names in order from the longest jump to the shortest jump.

_____

_____

_____

6. How many total inches did Gwen, Leon, and Brady jump? Write a number sentence to show your answer.

_____

_____

Spiral Review and Test Prep 4-1

Circle the correct answer.

Add.

1.
$$\begin{array}{r} 373 \\ +\ 496 \\ \hline \end{array}$$

    A. 869
    B. 877
    C. 879
    D. 886

2.
$$\begin{array}{r} 782 \\ +\ 577 \\ \hline \end{array}$$

    A. 1,258
    B. 1,356
    C. 1,359
    D. 1,392

3. Which number makes the equation true?

$38 + \underline{\hspace{1cm}} = 40$

    A. 0   **C.** 2
    B. 1   **D.** 3

4. Round 407 to the nearest ten.

    A. 400   **C.** 500
    B. 410   **D.** 510

Subtract.

5. $700 - 512 =$ _____

6. $832 - 18 =$ _____

7. Esther made a necklace of beads. She used the pattern green, green, green, yellow, yellow, and yellow. She used 30 beads to make the necklace. How many green beads did she use? Draw a picture to solve the problem and write your answer.

_____

_____

© Pearson Education, Inc. 3

Spiral Review and Test Prep 4-2

● Circle the correct answer.

1. $36.72
        − 14.18

   A. $22.54
   B. $22.56
   C. $22.64
   D. $22.66

2. What time is shown on the clock?

   A. 3:07   C. 7:03
   B. 3:35   D. 7:15

3. Subtract.

        455
      − 278

   A. 167
   B. 177
   C. 187
   D. 197

States & Area

State	Area in Square Miles
Minnesota	84,402
Iowa	56,290
California	158,706
Pennsylvania	45,308
Texas	266,807

4. About how many square miles of land do Minnesota and California have together? Is an estimate enough? Explain.

_____

_____

_____

_____

_____

5. Solve the problem.

_____

Spiral Review and Test Prep 4-3

Circle the correct answer.

1. Alice bought an 8 oz can of fruit juice. The number 8 on the can is for

    A. measuring.
    B. counting.
    C. locating.
    D. naming.

2. What time is shown on the clock?

    A. 3:17   **C.** 9:15
    B. 3:46   **D.** 9:18

3. What is the value of the 3 in 563,720?

    A. 30   **C.** 3,000
    B. 300   **D.** 30,000

Subtract.

4.
$$\begin{array}{r} 307 \\ -\ 114 \\ \hline \end{array}$$

5.
$$\begin{array}{r} 620 \\ -\ 369 \\ \hline \end{array}$$

6. Dan can pack 6 boxes in 1 hr. Draw a picture to show how many boxes he could pack in 4 hr and write your answer.

_____

_____

Spiral Review and Test Prep 4-4

Circle the correct answer.

1. Add.

416
+ 123

A. 313
B. 533
C. 539
D. 549

2. Subtract.

234
+ 188

A. 56
B. 52
C. 46
D. 42

3. A baby blue whale is 25 ft long at birth. A baby giraffe is 6 ft tall at birth. Which expression shows the difference between the baby whale's length and the baby giraffe's height?

A. 25 + 6
B. 2 + 5 + 6
C. 25 − 6
D. 25 − 7

Find the elapsed time.

4. Start time: 10:30 P.M.

End time: 1:15 A.M.

_____

5. The highest point in South Dakota is Harney Peak, at 7,242 ft. South Dakota's lowest point is 962 ft, at Big Stone Lake. How much greater is the height of Harney Peak than Big Stone Lake? Is an estimate enough to solve this problem? Explain.

_____

_____

_____

_____

6. Solve the problem.

_____

Spiral Review and Test Prep 4-5

Circle the correct answer.

1. Which digit is in the thousands place?

49,316

A. 9   **C.** 3
B. 4   **D.** 1

2. Which of the following completes this pattern?

78, 80, 82, _____, _____

A. 84, 82   **C.** 84, 86
B. 86, 84   **D.** 84, 88

3. Which of the following makes the number sentence true?

$7 + b > 12$

A. $b = 3$ **C.** $b = 5$
B. $b = 4$ **D.** $b = 6$

4. Subtract.

$$\begin{array}{r} 517 \\ -\ 238 \\ \hline \end{array}$$

A. 271
B. 279
C. 321
D. 371

November 2000

S	M	T	W	Th	F	S
			1	2	3	4
5	6	7	8	9	10	11
12	13	14	15	16	17	18
19	20	21	22	23	24	25
26	27	28	29	30		

5. On what day of the week was November 13, 2000?

_____

6. Nancy has swimming lessons on Mondays and Wednesdays. How many times did she go to swimming lessons in November 2000?

_____

_____

_____

_____

_____

© Pearson Education, Inc. 3

Spiral Review and Test Prep 4-6

Circle the correct answer.

Student Bedtimes	
8:30 P.M.	~~HHH~~ III
9:00 P.M.	~~HHH~~ ~~HHH~~ IIII
9:30 P.M.	IIII

1. Use mental math to find the sum.

33 + 52

A. 67   **C.** 85
B. 81   **D.** 87

2. How many sides does a square have?

A. 3   **C.** 5
B. 4   **D.** 6

3. Which number is greater than 1,101?

A. 1,001   **C.** 1,100
B. 1,011   **D.** 1,110

4. Jim begins jogging at 6:45 A.M. He finishes at 8:00 A.M. For how long did he jog?

A. 1 hr
B. 1 hr, 15 min
C. 1 hr, 30 min
D. 2 hr

5. How many students have a 9:00 P.M. bedtime?

_____

6. Does the chart show an exact number or an estimate? Explain.

_____

_____

_____

Subtract.

7. $79.05
   −   43.67

8. $85.00
   −   32.16

Spiral Review and Test Prep 4-7

Circle the correct answer.

1. Alice rounded 14,378 to 14,400. To what place did she round?

- **A.** Tens
- **B.** Hundreds
- **C.** Thousands
- **D.** Ten thousands

Add.

2.
$$\begin{array}{r} 63 \\ + 48 \\ \hline \end{array}$$

- **A.** 111
- **B.** 125
- **C.** 128
- **D.** 132

3.
$$\begin{array}{r} 199 \\ + 622 \\ \hline \end{array}$$

- **A.** 721
- **B.** 722
- **C.** 821
- **D.** 822

4. The rule is Subtract 6. Which number does Jim get if he puts in 9?

- **A.** 2
- **C.** 15
- **B.** 3
- **D.** 18

5. Thomas Edison set up a laboratory with the hope of producing a new invention every 10 days. Draw a picture to show how many inventions could have been produced in 80 days and write your answer.

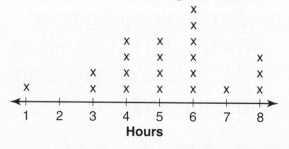

Time Spent Watching Television

6. What is the mode for this data?

_____

Name_____

Spiral Review and Test Prep 4-8

● Circle the correct answer.

1. Which number makes the number sentence true?

$122 + n < 140$

A. $n = 17$ **C.** $n = 21$
B. $n = 19$ **D.** $n = 23$

2. Round to the nearest hundred to estimate the sum.

$642 + 197$

A. 600 **C.** 800
B. 700 **D.** 900

3. Which of the following is equal to 3 tens, 16 ones?

A. 36 **C.** 56
B. 46 **D.** 66

4. There are 9 people ahead of Ralph. He is the ____ person in line.

A. 8th **C.** 10th
B. 9th **D.** 11th

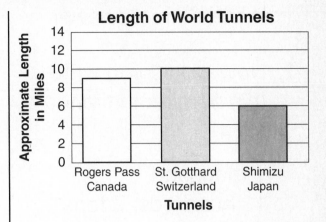

Length of World Tunnels

5. About how long is the Rogers Pass tunnel?

_____

6. Jason wants to donate $7.00 to the soup kitchen. He has saved $4.93. How much more money does he need? Is an estimate enough? Explain.

_____

_____

_____

_____

7. Solve the problem.

_____

Spiral Review and Test Prep 4-9

Circle the correct answer.

1. How would you write this number in standard form?

1 thousand,
11 hundreds, 7 tens

A. 11,170   **C.** 2,170
B. 2,270   **D.** 1,270

Add.

2. $11.73
    +   4.14

A. $12.87   **C.** $15.87
B. $15.81   **D.** $15.97

3. $0.55
    +   8.99

A. $8.54   **C.** $9.54
B. $8.55   **D.** $9.55

4. Round 5,729 to the nearest hundred.

A. 5,700   **C.** 5,800
B. 5,730   **D.** 5,830

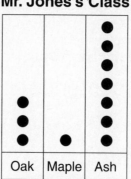
Mr. Jones's Class

| Oak | Maple | Ash |

Each ● = 2 votes.

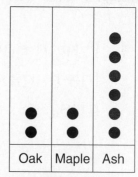
Mrs. Smith's Class

| Oak | Maple | Ash |

Each ● = 2 votes.

5. Write two statements about how the two groups are alike.

_____

_____

_____

_____

6. Austin had 98 stickers. He traded 10 stickers for 7 new stickers. How many does he have now? Is an estimate enough? Explain.

_____

_____

_____

Spiral Review and Test Prep 4-10

Circle the correct answer.

1. Delia paid for $4.78 worth of groceries with a $5.00 bill. What was her change?

A. 2 nickels, 2 pennies
B. 2 dimes, 2 pennies
C. 1 nickel, 1 dime, 1 penny
D. 1 nickel, 2 dimes, 2 pennies

Add or subtract.

2. $14.87
      +   39.90

A. $23.05   **C.** $54.77
B. $25.03   **D.** $55.77

3.   1,362
      −   859

A. 503   **C.** 2,221
B. 521   **D.** 2,231

Write the ordered pair that describes the location of each point.

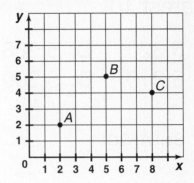

4. Point A _____

5. Point B _____

6. Point C _____

7. An adult jack rabbit can leap 20 ft in a single jump. Draw a picture to show how far an adult jack rabbit could leap in four jumps and write your answer.

Spiral Review and Test Prep 4-11

Circle the correct answer.

1. Round 5,316 to the nearest 10.

   A. 5,320   **C.** 5,306

   B. 5,310   **D.** 5,300

Add or subtract.

2.   307
       121
   + 677

   A. 1,012   **C.** 1,105

   B. 1,015   **D.** 1,212

3. $561.87
  −   103.32

   A. $358.45 **C.** $559.65

   B. $458.55 **D.** $665.19

4. Complete the pattern.

132, 122, 112, ____, ____

   A. 122, 132

   B. 102, 92

   C. 92, 102

   D. 102, 82

5. Pete has 34 books, and Tim has 16 books. How many more books does Pete have than Tim? Is an estimate enough? Explain.

_____

_____

_____

6. Solve the problem.

_____

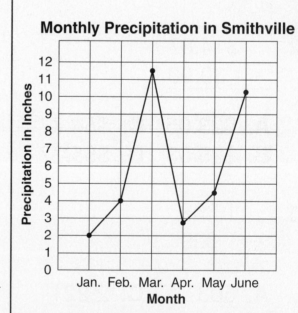

Monthly Precipitation in Smithville

7. How much precipitation did Smithville receive in January?

_____

Name_____

Spiral Review and Test Prep 4-12

Circle the correct answer.

1. Which number is the same as 10 tens and 6 ones?

   A. 16   **C.** 106
   B. 60   **D.** 116

2. How much money is 6 quarters, 5 dimes, and 2 nickels?

   A. $2.10
   B. $1.85
   C. $1.70
   D. $1.55

3. Which number makes the number sentence true?

   $13 - n > 9$

   A. 3   **C.** 5
   B. 4   **D.** 6

Felix has 3 more hats than Bill. If Bill has 7 hats, how many hats does Felix have?

4. What operation will you use to solve this problem?

_____

3rd-Grade Hair Color

Color	Tally	Number
Brown	~~卌卌~~ l	11
Red	llll	4
Black	~~卌卌~~ llll	14
Blonde	~~卌卌卌~~ l	16

5. Use color to make a pictograph of the data in the table.

Spiral Review and Test Prep 4-13

Circle the correct answer.

1. $155 + 89 + 62 =$ ___

    A. 289   **C.** 310

    B. 306   **D.** 319

2. Gregory has a penny. What are his chances of flipping the coin and it landing heads up?

    A. 1 out of 2

    B. 1 out of 3

    C. 2 out of 3

    D. 3 out of 4

3. $(4 + 18) + 7 =$ ___ $+ 7$

    A. 418   **C.** 41

    B. 48   **D.** 22

4.   749
      $-$ 562
      _____

    A. 187   **C.** 189

    B. 188   **D.** 1,311

Books Read in Class

Type of Book	Number Read
Mystery	18
Nonfiction	21
Fantasy	16
Poetry	9

5. Use the data to make a bar graph.

6. What is the total number of mystery and fantasy books the class read? Is an estimate enough to solve this problem?

_____

_____

© Pearson Education, Inc. 3

Spiral Review and Test Prep 4-14

Circle the correct answer.

1.
$$\begin{array}{r} 19 \\ + 48 \\ \hline \end{array}$$

A. 57
B. 67
C. 69
D. 72

2. 4 thousands, 2 tens, 5 ones = _____

A. 4,025   **C.** 4,225
B. 4,205   **D.** 4,250

3.
$$\begin{array}{r} 502 \\ - 67 \\ \hline \end{array}$$

A. 435   **C.** 455
B. 445   **D.** 569

4. Round 7,605 to the nearest 10.

A. 7,600   **C.** 7,615
B. 7,610   **D.** 7,620

5. Jan read 97 books, Mary read 91, and Steve read 103. About how many books did they read? Is an estimate enough? Explain.

_____

_____

_____

_____

Points Scored by Quarter

Quarter	Points Scored
First	3
Second	7
Third	10
Fourth	8

6. Plot the points for the number of points scored.

Points Scored by Quarter

Spiral Review and Test Prep 4-15

Circle the correct answer.

Find each difference.

1.   218   **A.** 66
    − 142   **B.** 69
               C. 76
               D. 79

2.   129   **A.** 87
    −   32   **B.** 89
               C. 92
               D. 97

3. Juan left for school at 7:15 A.M. and arrived home at 4:00 P.M. How long was he away from home?

    A. 7 hr, 15 min
    B. 7 hr, 45 min
    C. 8 hr, 15 min
    D. 8 hr, 45 min

The school soccer team has enough jerseys for 21 players. How many more jerseys would the school need if 30 students wanted to be on the soccer team?

4. Solve. Is an estimate enough? Explain.

    _____

    _____

    _____

    _____

5. Use the data to complete the line plot.

Number of Situps Done by Fourth Graders
11 8 8 10 8 7 3 8 4 6 6 8 5 10

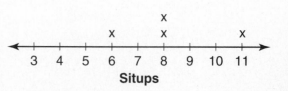

Situps

Name_____

Spiral Review and Test Prep 5-1

Circle the correct answer.

1. Han began jogging at 7:15 and stopped at 8:10. For how long did he jog?

A. 45 min
B. 55 min
C. 1 hr, 5 min
D. 1 hr, 15 min

2.

What time is shown on the clock?

A. 1:30   **C.** 6:05
B. 12:30   **D.** 7:05

3. Which phrase means the same as 3:45?

A. Half past three
B. Quarter to three
C. Fifteen minutes to four
D. Quarter after four

Dog Heights

Dog	Average Adult Height
German shepherd	25 in.
Fox terrier	15 in.
Golden retriever	23 in.

4. Use the information in the chart to complete the bar graph.

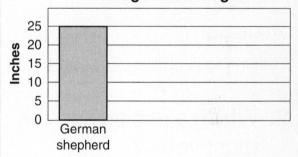

5. What is the height of the three dogs combined?

_____

6. Write 500 + 70 + 3 in standard form.

_____

Spiral Review and Test Prep 5-2

Circle the correct answer.

1. Which sentence shows 5 groups of 6?

 A. 5×6

 B. $5 + 6$

 C. $5 + 5 + 5 + 5 + 5$

 D. $6 \times 6 \times 6 \times 6 \times 6$

Number of Clay Models Made by Art Club Members in May				
8	6	6	6	2
5	8	8	5	5
4	6	6	3	7

4. Use the data above to complete the line plot.

Favorite Exercise

Push-ups	ЖЖ
Sit-ups	II
Aerobics	ЖЖ III
Running	ЖЖ I

2. Which exercise had the most votes?

 A. Push-ups

 B. Sit-ups

 C. Aerobics

 D. Running

3. How many people were surveyed?

 A. 5   **C.** 21

 B. 15   **D.** 25

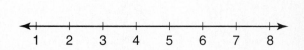

5. How many art club members made five clay models in May?

_____

6. Estimate the difference.

$303 - 121$

_____

Spiral Review and Test Prep 5-3

Circle the correct answer.

○ ○ ○ ○ ○ ○ ○
○ ○ ○ ○ ○ ○ ○
○ ○ ○ ○ ○ ○ ○
○ ○ ○ ○ ○ ○ ○

1. Which multiplication fact is shown by the array?

A. 4×6 **C.** 7×3

B. 5×7 **D.** 4×7

2. Subtract.

$$\begin{array}{r} 84 \\ -\ 17 \\ \hline \end{array}$$

A. 53
B. 66
C. 67
D. 101

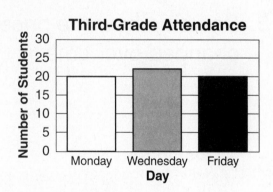

Third-Grade Attendance

Number of Students

30
25
20
15
10
5
0

Monday   Wednesday   Friday
Day

3. How many third graders attended school on Friday?

A. 15 **C.** 25
B. 20 **D.** 30

Points Scored in Basketball Game	
Ray	9
Steve	2
Mary	7
Tim	10

4. Use the data above to complete the pictograph.

Points Scored in Basketball Game

Ray	

Each ○ = 2 points

5. Which player scored the most points?

_____

6. $6 \times$ _____ $= 30$

$5 \times$ _____ $= 30$

Spiral Review and Test Prep 5-4

Circle the correct answer.

Mr. Jackson bought 3 tennis-ball containers. Each container had 3 balls. How many tennis balls did Mr. Jackson buy?

1. Which number sentence relates to the multiplication story above?

A. 3 + 3 = 6

B. 3 × 3 × 3 = 27

C. 3 + 3 + 3 + 3 = 12

D. 3 × 3 = 9

2. Gary has 3 quarters and 5 dimes. How much money does he have?

A. $1.05   **C.** $1.25

B. $1.15   **D.** $1.55

3. Add mentally.

14 + 30 =

A. 16   **C.** 34

B. 26   **D.** 44

Typical Cost of a Magazine

Year	Price
1966	$0.35
1976	$1.50
1986	$2.50
1996	$3.95

4. Use the data above to complete the line graph.

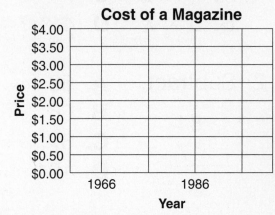

5. Describe how the price changed over time.

_____

6.

Write the time shown on the clock.

_____

Spiral Review and Test Prep 5-5

Circle the correct answer.

October 2002						
S	M	T	W	T	F	S
		1	2	3	4	5
6	7	8	9	10	11	12
13	14	15	16	17	18	19
20	21	22	23	24	25	26
27	28	29	30	31		

1. What day of the week was October 30, 2002?

   A. Monday
   B. Tuesday
   C. Wednesday
   D. Thursday

2. How many Thursdays were there in October 2002?

   A. 3   **C.** 5
   B. 4   **D.** 6

3. Kiley bought $2.47 worth of fabric and paid with a $5.00 bill. How much change did she get?

   A. $2.53   **C.** $3.53
   B. $2.63   **D.** $3.63

4. Dave placed 5 peanuts in each baggie. How many peanuts did he place in 6 baggies? Complete the table for this problem.

Baggie	1	2	3	4	5	6
Peanuts	5					

5. Solve the problem.

_____

6. Joe's Bakery sold 2 cakes on Tuesday, 8 on Wednesday, 12 on Thursday, and 16 on Friday. Use this data to complete the pictograph.

Joe's Bakery

Day	Cakes Sold
Tuesday	
Wednesday	
Thursday	
Friday	

Each ☐ = 4 cakes

Spiral Review and Test Prep 5-6

Circle the correct answer.

1. Multiply.

$$\begin{array}{r} 2 \\ \times\ \$8 \\ \hline \end{array}$$

A. $4
B. $6
C. $10
D. $16

2. What is the product of 9 and 2?

A. 7   **C.** 16
B. 11   **D.** 18

3. Subtract.

$$\begin{array}{r} 230 \\ -\ 186 \\ \hline \end{array}$$

A. 44
B. 54
C. 144
D. 416

4. Which shape has only three sides?

A. Triangle
B. Square
C. Pentagon
D. Hexagon

5. Use the data to complete the line plot.

Gift-Wrapped Packages Sold by Third Graders			
26	25	26	24
26	22	23	24
21	21	21	22
26	25	22	27

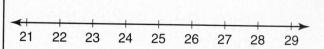

21 22 23 24 25 26 27 28 29

6. How many students sold fewer than 26 packages?

_____

7. What is the range of the data?

_____

Name_____

Spiral Review and Test Prep 5-7

Circle the correct answer.

1. The orchestra concert lasted from 7:05 to 9:35. How long was the concert?

A. 2 hr, 15 min
B. 2 hr, 25 min
C. 2 hr, 30 min
D. 2 hr, 35 min

2. $5 \times$ _____ $= 45$

A. 3   C. 7
B. 5   D. 9

3. Which two factors, when multiplied, have a product of 25?

A. 5 and 2
B. 2 and 10
C. 5 and 5
D. 5 and 10

4. What is $\square + 15$ if $\square = 20$?

A. 5   C. 35
B. 20   D. 45

5. Use the chart to complete the line graph.

Mara's Homework

Day	Homework Time
Monday	75 min.
Tuesday	60 min.
Wednesday	45 min.
Thursday	30 min.

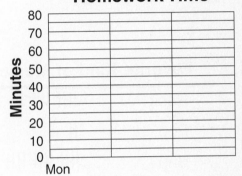

Homework Time

6. How did the time Mara spent on homework change between Monday and Thursday?

_____

7. Order the numbers from least to greatest.

17, 35, 110, 88, 2

_____

Spiral Review and Test Prep 5-8

Circle the correct answer.

1. 10 × 7 =

   A. 50   **C.** 70

   B. 60   **D.** 80

2. 10 × _____ = 40

   A. 2   **C.** 6

   B. 4   **D.** 8

3.

Favorite Kind of Music	
Rock	卌 卌 I
Pop	II
Rap	卌 卌 IIII
Classical	卌 I

Based on the survey, which kind of music was the least popular?

   A. Rock   **C.** Pop

   B. Rap   **D.** Classical

4. What is the product of 5 and 9?

   A. 4   **C.** 45

   B. 14   **D.** 56

5. Use the data in the chart to complete the bar graph.

Third-Grade Test Scores

Student	Score
Wanda	95
Bill	85
Wade	75

Third-Grade Test Scores

6. How many points higher did Wanda score on the test than Wade?

_____

7. What ordinal number comes before 8th?

_____

Spiral Review and Test Prep 5-9

Circle the correct answer.

1. Myron bought 4 books on Monday and 3 books on Tuesday. Each book cost $4, including tax. How much money did he spend on the books?

A. $11   **C.** $26

B. $18   **D.** $28

2.

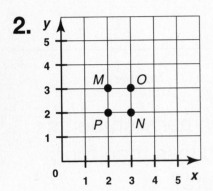

Which point is located at (3, 2)?

A. Point *M*   **C.** Point *O*

B. Point *N*   **D.** Point *P*

3. Multiply.

$$\begin{array}{r} \$10 \\ \times \quad 6 \\ \hline \end{array}$$

A. $16

B. $26

C. $60

D. $120

4. Use the data to complete the pictograph.

Sales at Elmer's Autos for One Week

Salesperson	Total Sales
Dave	$5,000
Chris	$2,000
Julie	$8,000
Jonathan	$3,000

Sales at Elmer's Autos for One Week

Dave	
Chris	
Julie	
Jonathan	

Each 🚗 = $2,000

5. Which salesperson sold the most during the week?

_____

Name_____

Spiral Review and Test Prep 5-10

Circle the correct answer.

1. $389 \times 1 =$

  A. 0   **C.** 388
  B. 1   **D.** 389

2. $0 \times 55 =$

  A. 0   **C.** 55
  B. 1   **D.** 550

3.

What time is shown on the clock?

  A. 12:33   **C.** 6:01
  B. 12:34   **D.** 6:02

4. Used CDs cost $3 each. Jim bought three and Pam bought four. How much money total did they spend?

  A. $7   **C.** $18
  B. $15   **D.** $21

5. Use the data to complete the line plot.

Data File

Number of Folders Used by Third Graders			
6	6	4	7
7	5	4	8
6	5	3	6
7	5	5	4

Folders Used by Third Graders

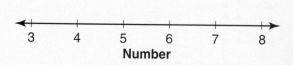

6. How many students used less than four folders?

_____

7. Write the fact family for 4 and 7.

_____

_____

8. Find the sum using mental math.

$17 + 40 =$ _____

Spiral Review and Test Prep 5-11

Circle the correct answer.

1. 7 × $9 =

A. $16   C. $63

B. $56   D. $79

2. Mario can fold 4 paper airplanes in 1 minute. How many can he fold in 9 minutes?

A. 27   C. 45

B. 36   D. 54

Favorite Vehicles of Mr. Verona's Class

SUVs	○○○○○○○
Sports cars	◐
Sedans	●●●
Station wagons	●●◗

Each ○ = 2 votes

3. How many more students preferred SUVs than station wagons?

A. 5   C. 14

B. 9   D. 19

4. Use the data to complete the line graph.

Number of Plants Grown Indoors	
Summer	0
Fall	5
Winter	15

Plants Grown Indoors

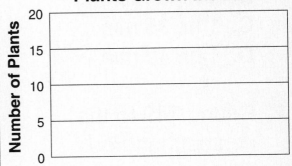

5. Did the number of plants grown indoors increase or decrease from fall to winter?

6. A bag has 100 red chips and 2 yellow chips. You grab 1 chip from the bag without looking. What color chip will you most likely grab?

Spiral Review and Test Prep 5-12

Circle the correct answer.

1. The meeting began at 8:15 and ended at 9:55. For how long did the meeting last?

   A. 40 min

   B. 1 hr, 5 min

   C. 1 hr, 35 min

   D. 1 hr, 40 min

2. Round 749 to the nearest hundred.

   A. 700   **C.** 750

   B. 740   **D.** 800

3. Add.

$$\begin{array}{r} \$15.88 \\ + \quad 7.99 \\ \hline \end{array}$$

   A. $22.87

   B. $22.88

   C. $23.87

   D. $23.88

4. Which of the following answers would be an overestimate for 67 + 55?

   A. 100   **C.** 115

   B. 110   **D.** 135

5. Use the data to complete the bar graph.

Standing Long Jump	
Mariah	36 in.
Thor	48 in.
Evelyn	21 in.

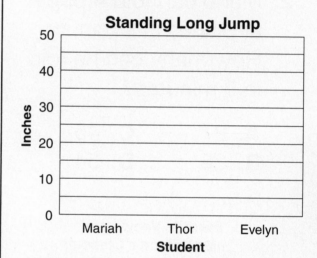

Standing Long Jump

6. Which student jumped the fewest inches?

_____

7. $5 \times 6 =$ _____

8. $4 \times 0 =$ _____

9. $1 \times 9 =$ _____

10. $9 \times 8 =$ _____

Spiral Review and Test Prep 6-1

Circle the correct answer.

1. Which of the following is NOT a multiple of 9?

A. 18   **C.** 62

B. 45   **D.** 72

2. Multiply.

$$\begin{array}{r} 10 \\ \times\ \$5 \\ \hline \end{array}$$

A. $15

B. $25

C. $50

D. $100

3. Which number is greater than 5,028?

A. 5,128   **C.** 5,008

B. 5,018   **D.** 4,998

4. Pedro helps his father each Saturday from 9:00 A.M. to 2:15 P.M. For how long does he help his father?

A. 5 hr

B. 5 hr, 10 min

C. 5 hr, 15 min

D. 6 hr

Complete the table to solve the problem.

5. Clara's father pays her an allowance of $6.50 per week. How much money will she have after 4 weeks?

Clara's Allowance

Number of weeks	1	2	3	4
Money received	$6.50	$13.00		

_____

_____

_____

Complete. You may use counters or draw a picture to help.

6. $6 \times 5 = 30$

_____ $\times\ 6 = 30$

7. $4 \times 7 = 28$

_____ $\times\ 4 = 28$

Spiral Review and Test Prep 6-2

Circle the correct answer.

1. Walter is 34th in line. Roland is behind him in line. What place in line is Roland?

A. 33rd   **C.** 35th
B. 34th   **D.** 36th

2. Round 507 to the nearest hundred.

A. 510   **C.** 410
B. 500   **D.** 400

3. Which of the following is a multiplication sentence for "three groups of four"?

A. $3 \times 4 = 12$
B. $3 + 3 + 3 = 9$
C. $4 + 3 = 7$
D. $4 \times 4 \times 4 = 64$

4. Which number makes the number sentence true? $8 - n < 6$

A. 3   **C.** 1
B. 2   **D.** 0

Write and answer the hidden question. Then solve the problem.

5. Rene bought 3 pairs of socks. Tim bought 5 pairs. Each pair cost $5. How much did they spend?

_____

_____

_____

_____

Multiply.

6. $3 \times 7 =$ _____

7. $3 \times 3 =$ _____

Complete.

○ ○ ○ ○ ○
○ ○ ○ ○ ○

8. 2 groups of _____

_____ + _____ $= 10$

$2 \times$ _____ $=$ _____

Spiral Review and Test Prep 6-3

● Circle the correct answer.

1. Multiply.

$$\begin{array}{r} 6 \\ \times\ 4 \\ \hline \end{array}$$

A. 10 **C.** 24
B. 12 **D.** 30

2.
$$\begin{array}{r} 0 \\ \times\ 3 \\ \hline \end{array}$$

A. 0 **C.** 3
B. 1 **D.** 13

3.

What is the name of this shape?

A. Hexagon
B. Triangle
C. Square
D. Rectangle

Write and answer the hidden question. Then solve the problem.

4. From Monday through Wednesday, Henry played a total of 7 hr with Tom. Henry played with Tom for 2 hr on Monday and 3 hr on Tuesday. How many hours did Henry play with Tom on Wednesday?

_____

_____

_____

_____

_____

Write <, >, or = for each _____.

5. 9×1 _____ 4×2

6. 1×0 _____ 0×25

Spiral Review and Test Prep 6-4

Circle the correct answer.

1. Clarice has 2 quarters, 2 dimes, and 1 nickel. How much money does she have?

A. $0.75   **C.** $0.50

B. $0.65   **D.** $0.45

2. Which number sentence shows the Associative (Grouping) Property of Addition?

A. $4 + 0 = 4$

B. $(7 + 2) + 3 = 7 + (2 + 3)$

C. $1 + 6 = 7$

D. $4 + 3 = 3 + 4$

Multiply.

3. $10 \times 9 =$

A. 18   **C.** 80

B. 19   **D.** 90

4. $5 \times 6 =$

A. 11   **C.** 30

B. 21   **D.** 40

Complete the table to solve the problem.

5. Jan is making a four-sided design using toothpicks. Each side of the design uses 11 toothpicks. How many toothpicks will Jan need to complete the design?

Sides	1	2	3	4
Toothpicks	11	22		

_____

_____

_____

_____

6. Find the product of 6 and 9.

_____

7. Multiply 7 and 3.

_____

Name_____

Spiral Review and Test Prep 6-5

● Circle the correct answer.

1. Which is seventy-five thousand, two hundred sixty-four in standard form?

    A. 75,264
    B. 75,254
    C. 72,264
    D. 72,254

Multiply.

● **2.** $10 \times 10 =$

    A. 20   **C.** 110
    B. 100   **D.** 200

3. $8 \times 7 =$

    A. 15   **C.** 56
    B. 16   **D.** 64

4. $\$2 \times 8 =$

    A. $10   **C.** $21
    B. $16   **D.** $28

Write and answer the hidden question. Then solve the problem.

5. Taylor purchased 8 "Thank You" cards. Maurice purchased 5 "Thank You" cards. Each card cost $2. How much money did the boys spend on the cards?

_____

_____

_____

6. What is the product of 5 and 9?

_____

7. Write the numbers in order from least to greatest.

    301   103   303   101

_____

Spiral Review and Test Prep 6-6

Circle the correct answer.

1. $9 \times 7 =$

A. 72 C. 56

B. 63 D. 54

2. $\begin{array}{r} 7 \\ \times\ 6 \\ \hline \end{array}$

A. 42 C. 56

B. 48 D. 64

3. If there are 6 groups of 8 sports cards, how many sports cards are there?

A. 10 C. 40

B. 14 D. 48

4. Which of the following is NOT a multiple of 2?

A. 9 C. 22

B. 18 D. 86

Complete the table to solve the problem. Write the answer in a complete sentence.

5. Thomas can paint 3 windows per day. How many windows can he paint in 5 days?

Days	1	2	3	4	5
Windows	3	6			

_____

_____

6. Write the fact family for 3 and 9.

_____

_____

Find each sum using mental math.

7. $29 + 33 =$ _____

8. $42 + 26 =$ _____

Spiral Review and Test Prep 6-7

Circle the correct answer.

What are the next 3 numbers in the pattern?

1. 45, 41, 37, ___, ___, ___

    A. 39, 43, 47
    B. 33, 29, 25
    C. 35, 31, 27
    D. 35, 30, 35

2. 55, 50, 45, 40, 35, ___, ___, ___

    A. 30, 35, 40
    B. 30, 25, 20
    C. 15, 20, 25
    D. 35, 45, 55

Number of Poems Written

Sue	○ ○
Batista	○ ○ ○
Rick	○ ○ ◖

Each ○ = 2 poems

3. How many poems did Rick write?

    A. 2   **C.** 4
    B. 3   **D.** 5

Write and answer the hidden question. Then solve the problem.

Lumber Prices	
Planks	$3.00
Plywood	$4.50
Shims	$0.75

4. Nick purchased 3 planks on Monday and 6 on Saturday. He purchased 2 pieces of plywood on Sunday. How much money did Nick spend on planks?

_____

_____

_____

_____

Write $<$, $>$, or $=$ for each ___.

5. 17×1 ___ 0×17

6. 0×66 ___ 45×0

7. 34×0 ___ 1×6

Spiral Review and Test Prep 6-8

Circle the correct answer.

1. Mark has 3 fruit rolls. Tina has twice as many fruit rolls as Mark. How many fruit rolls does Tina have?

A. 3   **C.** 9

B. 6   **D.** 12

2. Which two factors could you multiply to get a product of 45?

A. 5 and 8   **C.** 5 and 7

B. 9 and 5   **D.** 9 and 8

3. $2 \times 8 =$

A. 16   **C.** 24

B. 20   **D.** 32

4.   84
   − 26
   _____

A. 52

B. 56

C. 58

D. 68

Complete the table to solve the problem.

5. Ichabod has $5. If he doubles the amount of money he has each day, how much money will he have after 4 days?

Days	1	2	3	4
Amount of money	$5	$10		

_____

_____

_____

6. Nikki is 5 times as old as Melinda, who is 2 years old. How old is Nikki?

_____

Spiral Review and Test Prep 6-9

Circle the correct answer.

1. Which number sentence shows the Commutative (Order) Property of Multiplication?

A. $2 + 4 = 4 + 2$
B. $3 \times 5 = (2 + 1) \times 5$
C. $6 \times 7 = 7 \times 6$
D. $(2 \times 4) = 8$

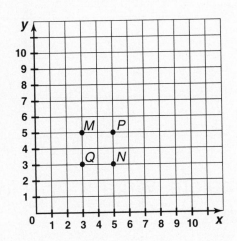

2. What point is located at (3, 5)?

A. Point M
B. Point N
C. Point P
D. Point Q

Write and answer the hidden question. Then solve the problem.

3. Tickets to the show cost $10. Terrence wants to go to the show with 2 friends. How much total will the group pay?

_____

_____

_____

Multiply.

4. $\begin{array}{r} 11 \\ \times\ 7 \\ \hline \end{array}$

5. $\begin{array}{r} 12 \\ \times\ 5 \\ \hline \end{array}$

6. What is the product of 5 and 6?

_____

Spiral Review and Test Prep 6-10

Circle the correct answer.

□

1. What is the name of the above shape?

   A. Rectangle
   B. Triangle
   C. Square
   D. Trapezoid

Multiply.

2. $5 \times 0 \times 3 =$

   A. 0   **C.** 5
   B. 3   **D.** 15

3. $4 \times 2 \times 1 =$

   A. 9   **C.** 7
   B. 8   **D.** 6

Complete the table to solve the problem.

4. The pet shop had 80 fish. It sold 8 fish each day. How many fish were left after 6 days?

Day	1	2	3	4	5	6
Fish	80					

_____

_____

_____

_____

Complete. Write $\times$ or $+$ for each _____.

5. 1 _____ 9 = 9

6. 5 _____ 0 = 5

7. 23 _____ 0 = 0

8. Find the sum using mental math.

   $56 + 16 =$ _____

Spiral Review and Test Prep 6-11

Circle the correct answer.

1. How would you write 500 + 70 + 9 in standard form?

A. 975   **C.** 759
B. 795   **D.** 579

2. Horace purchased a book for $2.95. He paid with a $5.00 bill. How much change will he receive?

A. $2.05   **C.** $3.15
B. $2.25   **D.** $3.35

3. What is the product of 9 × 9?

A. 9   **C.** 28
B. 18   **D.** 81

4. What is the product of 10 and 10?

A. 1,000   **C.** 20
B. 100   **D.** 10

Write and answer the hidden question. Then solve the problem.

5. Natalie earns $5 for each lawn she mows. She mowed 3 lawns on Saturday and 1 on Sunday. How much money did she earn?

_____

_____

_____

_____

_____

6. Write a rule for the table. Complete the table.

In	2	4	6	8	10
Out	6	12			

_____

_____

_____

Spiral Review and Test Prep 6-12

Circle the correct answer.

1. Round 83 to the nearest ten.

   A. 10   **C.** 80

   B. 50   **D.** 100

2. At the music store, new CDs cost $15 and used CDs cost $5. Sasha purchased 3 new CDs and 1 used CD. How much did Sasha spend?

   A. $50   **C.** $40

   B. $45   **D.** $35

3. $5 \times 7 =$

   A. 15   **C.** 35

   B. 25   **D.** 55

4. $\$10$
     $\times \quad 4$

   A. $14

   B. $40

   C. $44

   D. $54

Draw a picture to show the main idea. Then choose an operation and solve the problem.

Soccer Team

Player	Goals Scored
Mario	18
Fritz	7
Angel	12
Denny	2

5. How many more goals did Angel score than Denny?

Spiral Review and Test Prep 7-1

Circle the correct answer.

1. Multiply.

$8 \times 7 =$

A. 42   **C.** 56
B. 49   **D.** 63

2. Which of the following is a square number?

A. 7   **C.** 10
B. 9   **D.** 13

3. Find the number that makes the number sentence true.

$8 + n > 15$

A. 5   **C.** 7
B. 6   **D.** 8

4. Multiply.

$6 \times 2 \times 1 =$

A. 12   **C.** 18
B. 13   **D.** 24

Draw a picture to show the main idea. Then choose an operation and solve the problem.

5. Bamboo is one of the fastest-growing plants. Some tropical bamboos may grow as much as 24 in. in a day. How many inches would these kinds of bamboo grow in three days?

_____

6. A soccer team has 11 players. How many players are there on 3 soccer teams?

_____

Spiral Review and Test Prep 7-2

Circle the correct answer.

1. Three friends want to share 9 marbles equally. How many marbles will each friend have?

   A. 2   **C.** 4
   B. 3   **D.** 5

2. Find the pattern. What are the next three numbers?

   95, 90, 85, 80

   A. 75, 70, 65
   B. 70, 60, 50
   C. 75, 73, 71
   D. 75, 74, 73

3. Which number sentence shows that a spider has twice as many legs as a mouse?

   A. $2 \times 4 = 8$
   B. $3 \times 6 = 18$
   C. $2 \times 3 \times 3 = 18$
   D. $4 \times 4 = 16$

Draw a picture to show the main idea. Then choose an operation and solve the problem.

4. Samina has two pies. She wants to give an equal-sized piece of pie to 16 people. How many slices must she cut from each pie?

   _____

5. How can you use 2×6 to find 4×6? Explain.

   _____

   _____

   _____

   _____

Spiral Review and Test Prep 7-3

● Circle the correct answer.

1. Multiply.

$4 \times 7 =$

A. 21   **C.** 35

B. 28   **D.** 42

2. Rounding to the nearest hundred, estimate the sum.

$133 + 86 + 34$

A. 100   **C.** 300

B. 200   **D.** 400

3. Multiply.

$6 \times 8 \times 2 =$

A. 15   **C.** 22

B. 20   **D.** 96

4. How many times do you have to subtract 5 from 15 to divide 15 into 3 equal groups?

A. 2   **C.** 5

B. 3   **D.** 15

5. According to the U.S. Census Bureau, the People's Republic of China had a population of 1,273,111,290 people in the year 2001. In what places in the population do you find the digit 2?

_____

_____

_____

_____

6. There are 6 bowls and 12 oranges. How many oranges in each bowl?

_____

7. Write the next two numbers in the pattern.

57, 46, 35, _____, _____

© Pearson Education, Inc. 3

Spiral Review and Test Prep 7-4

Circle the correct answer.

1. What is the next number in the pattern?

21, 23, 25, 27

A. 26   C. 29

B. 28   D. 31

2. Multiply.

$9 \times 7 =$

A. 27   C. 54

B. 72   D. 63

3. The rule is add 23. If the **Out** number is 46, what is the **In** number?

A. 13   C. 26

B. 23   D. 33

4. There are 5 boxes and 20 hats. How many hats are in each box?

A. 15   C. 5

B. 10   D. 4

5. Write a division sentence to show how to solve the division story.

The distance between Chicago and Minneapolis is 409 mi. It takes about 8 hr to drive between the two cities. If a driver stopped every 2 hr to rest, how many times would the driver stop?

_____

_____

6. How many students had more than 2 siblings?

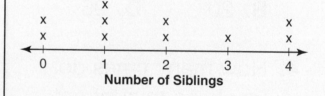

_____

Spiral Review and Test Prep 7-5

Circle the correct answer.

1. Multiply.

$6 \times 9 =$

A. 36   **C.** 49

B. 42   **D.** 54

2. Round 632,426 to the nearest ten thousand.

A. 630,000

B. 632,000

C. 632,400

D. 650,000

3. Multiply.

$\$8 \times 7 =$

A. $1   **C.** $49

B. $15   **D.** $56

4. Which numbers come next in the pattern?

145, 146, 126, 127

A. 144, 143

B. 128, 129

C. 148, 147

D. 107, 108

5 Longest Snakes

Snake	Greatest Length
Reticulated python	35 ft
Anaconda	28 ft
Indian python	25 ft
Diamond python	21 ft
King cobra	19 ft

5. Which three snakes, if lined up end to end, would have a total length of 68 ft?

_____

_____

_____

6. Write a division story for $16 \div 8$.

_____

_____

_____

_____

_____

_____

Spiral Review and Test Prep 7-6

Circle the correct answer.

1. Which of the following is FALSE?

   A. 461 < 561

   B. 94 > 99

   C. 1,235 > 1,233

   D. 4,924 = 4,924

2. A ranch has two times as many sheep as dairy cows. If the ranch has 32 dairy cows, how many sheep are on the ranch?

   A. 32   **C.** 64

   B. 50   **D.** 96

3. Multiply.

   $5 \times 1 \times 8 =$

   A. 48   **C.** 40

   B. 45   **D.** 14

4. Write the fact family for 6, 3, and 18.

_____

_____

_____

5.

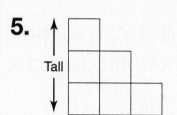

The picture shows a stairway built of blocks that are square. How wide would the stairway be if it was 6 steps tall?

_____

_____

6. Tina is twice as old as her cousin Sally. Their ages combined are 21. How old is each girl?

_____

Spiral Review and Test Prep 7-7

Circle the correct answer.

1. Multiply.

$8 \times 2 \times 3 =$

A. 16   **C.** 40
B. 24   **D.** 48

2. Dan saw 25 geese the first week, 50 geese the second week, and 75 geese the third week. If this pattern continues, how many geese will Dan see the fourth week?

A. 25   **C.** 125
B. 100   **D.** 150

3. Francine has 5 CDs. Millie has 3 times as many. How many CDs does Millie have?

A. 5   **C.** 10
B. 8   **D.** 15

4. Starfish most often have 5 arms. If an aquarium has 5-armed starfish and the total number of arms is 35, how many starfish are in the aquarium? How could you skip count to find 35 ÷ 5?

_____

_____

_____

_____

_____

_____

5. Write the fact family for 5, 8, and 40.

_____

_____

_____

_____

Spiral Review and Test Prep 7-8

Circle the correct answer.

1. What is the next number in the pattern?

565, 454, 343, _____

A. 656   **C.** 232

B. 434   **D.** 121

2. What has the same value as $3 \times 5 \times 2$?

A. 15×2

B. $3 \times 3 \times 4$

C. $3 + 5 + 2$

D. $3 \times 2 \times 10$

3. Which number can be divided equally by both 3 and 4?

A. 9   **C.** 20

B. 15   **D.** 24

4. Subtract.

$\begin{array}{r} \$5.19 \\ - \$1.73 \\ \hline \end{array}$

A. $3.24

B. $3.46

C. $3.51

D. $3.56

5. Find 35 divided by 5.

_____

6. Write the next three numbers in the pattern.

36, 40, 44, _____,

_____, _____

7.

Write the time shown on the clock in two ways.

_____

_____

Name_____

Spiral Review and Test Prep 7-9

Circle the correct answer.

1. Multiply.

$\$5 \times 3 =$

A. $12   **C.** $18
B. $15   **D.** $21

2. Divide 28 by 7.

A. 3   **C.** 5
B. 4   **D.** 6

3. How much money do you have if you have a ten-dollar bill, a one-dollar bill, five dimes, and two pennies?

A. $10.50
B. $10.52
C. $11.52
D. $11.70

4. Divide.

$3\overline{)24}$

A. 6   **C.** 12
B. 8   **D.** 21

Draw a picture to show the main idea. Then choose an operation and solve the problem.

5. Jerry works at a gas station and earns $9 per hour. How much does he earn if he works for 3 hr on Sunday?

_____

6. Show how you can use doubles to find 4×9.

_____

_____

_____

Multiply.

7. $9 \times 9 =$ _____

Spiral Review and Test Prep 7-10

Circle the correct answer.

1. What is the product of 6 and 9?

   A. 17   **C.** 54
   B. 36   **D.** 72

2. Which multiplication sentence will help you solve the problem?

   64 ÷ 8

   A. 8 × 3 = 24
   B. 8 × 5 = 40
   C. 8 × 6 = 48
   D. 8 × 8 = 64

3. What is the product of 0 and 3?

   A. 0   **C.** 3
   B. 1   **D.** 30

4. The Apollo-Saturn space program took U.S. astronauts to the moon. Each Apollo spacecraft carried 3 astronauts. 9 missions flew to the moon and back. How many U.S. astronauts flew to the moon? What operation did you use to solve the problem?

   _____

   _____

   _____

5. A dodgeball team has 7 players. In Juan's school, 63 students want to form a dodgeball league. How many teams can there be in the league?

   _____

Spiral Review and Test Prep 7-11

Circle the correct answer.

1. Use mental math.

$9 \times 7 =$

A. 63   **C.** 81

B. 72   **D.** 90

2. What is the pattern?

3, 15, 27, 39

A. Add 12, subtract 1
B. Add 12
C. Subtract 2, add 10
D. Multiply by 2

3. Which of the following is FALSE?

A. $0 \times 9 = 0$
B. $3 \times 0 = 1$
C. $0 \times 14 = 0$
D. $12 \times 1 = 12$

4. Divide.

$9\overline{)36}$

A. 4   **C.** 6

B. 5   **D.** 7

5. On a table of multiplication facts, could the number 81 appear in the 12s column? Explain.

_____

_____

6. Compare. Use $<$, $>$, or $=$.

$8 \div 8$ _____ $7 \div 1$

7.

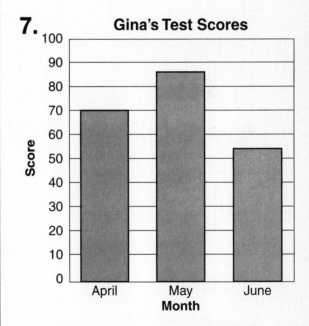

Gina's Test Scores

In which month did Gina score the highest?

_____

Spiral Review and Test Prep 7-12

Circle the correct answer.

April

S	M	T	W	T	F	S
						1
2	3	4	5	6	7	8
9	10	11	12	13	14	15
16	17	18	19	20	21	22
23/30	24	25	26	27	28	29

1. Which date is 2 weeks from April 6?

A. April 7
B. April 13
C. April 20
D. April 27

2. Divide.

$81 \div 8 =$

A. 9 R7
B. 9 R9
C. 10 R1
D. 10 R2

3. Multiply.

$6 \times 6 =$

A. 24   **C.** 48
B. 36   **D.** 60

4. If a cheetah ran at 75 km per hour and a human ran 25 km per hour, how many times faster than the person is the cheetah?

_____

_____

_____

_____

5. Compare. Use <, >, or =.

$6 \div 6 \bigcirc 0 \div 149$

6. Write the next two entries in the pattern.

G6, H7, I8, _____,

_____

Spiral Review and Test Prep 7-13

Circle the correct answer.

1. Divide.

$12\overline{)108}$ **A.** 8
               B. 9
               C. 10
               D. 11

2. Multiply.

$8 \times \$6 =$

A. $24   **C.** $42
B. $32   **D.** $48

3. What is another way of thinking of the number sentence 4×8?

A. $2 \times 8 + 2 \times 8$
B. $2 \times 4 + 2 \times 4$
C. $2 \times 4 + 4 \times 8$
D. $3 \times 4 + 3 \times 4$

4. If the rule is multiply by 6, and the **In** number is 8, what is the **Out** number?

A. 2   **C.** 36
B. 14   **D.** 48

Draw a picture to show the main idea. Then choose an operation and solve the problem.

5. Harry had 25 hooks in his fishing tackle box. He lost 8 of the hooks. How many hooks does he have left?

_____

6. Find the quotient and remainder.

$5\overline{)19}$

7. Josiah spent $3.56. He paid with a $10.00 bill. How much change should he receive?

Spiral Review and Test Prep 7-14

Circle the correct answer.

1. What is the product of 7 and 6?

A. 42   **C.** 13

B. 21   **D.** 1

2. Mario needs three times as many onions as peppers for his stew. If he needs 8 peppers, how many onions does he need?

A. 15   **C.** 21

B. 18   **D.** 24

3. Which numerical expression shows the word phrase *12 cartons of 12 eggs*?

A. 12 + 12

B. 144 − 12

C. 12 × 12

D. 12 ÷ 12

4. Draw the figure that comes next in the pattern.

△ + + ▯ ○ △ + _____

5. What is 110 divided by 11?

_____

Birds at the Feeder in 1 Hr	Tally	Number
Cardinals	III	3
Chickadees	ℋℋ	5
Blue jays	I	1
Goldfinches	II	2
Sparrows	ℋℋ IIII	9

6. Jim recorded the types of birds that visited his bird feeder in 1 hr. How many more chickadees were there than cardinals? _____

Name_____

Spiral Review and Test Prep 8-1

Circle the correct answer.

1. Divide.

30 ÷ 10 =

A. 2   **C.** 4
B. 3   **D.** 5

2. Which fact will help you find 28 ÷ 4?

A. 4 × 7 = 28
B. 2 × 12 = 24
C. 3 × 4 = 12
D. 3 × 7 = 21

3. Divide.

72 ÷ 8 =

A. 6   **C.** 8
B. 7   **D.** 9

4. Multiply.

2 × 11 =

A. 21   **C.** 33
B. 22   **D.** 45

Carrot Bread Alfred helped his mother bake loaves of carrot bread for a bake sale. They need 6 carrots to bake one loaf. A bunch of carrots has 10 carrots. How many loaves can Alfred and his mother bake with 3 bunches of carrots?

5. Try, check, and revise to solve the problem. Write your answer in a complete sentence.

_____

_____

_____

_____

6. Write an expression to show how to solve the problem.

_____

© Pearson Education, Inc. 3

Spiral Review and Test Prep 8-2

Circle the correct answer.

1. There are 24 books to place on 3 shelves. How many times must you subtract 3 from 24 to find 24 ÷ 3?

A. 6   **C.** 8
B. 7   **D.** 9

2. Divide.

66 ÷ 6 =

A. 12   **C.** 10
B. 11   **D.** 9

3.

Orange Juice

Name the solid figure.

A. Cube
B. Cylinder
C. Prism
D. Pyramid

Write a numerical expression for each word phrase.

4. the product of 7 and 25

_____

5. three times as large as 7 ft

_____

Try, check, and revise to solve the problem.

6. Paul needs to buy boxes of juice. Boxes of juice come in packs of 6. There are 23 people to serve. Paul says he needs 4 packs of boxes of juice. Is he right? Explain.

_____

_____

_____

_____

Spiral Review and Test Prep 8-3

● Circle the correct answer.

Try, check, and revise to solve the problem.

1. A bag contains 15 apples. If 5 friends want to share the apples equally, how many apples will each get?

A. 5   **C.** 3
B. 4   **D.** 2

2. Divide.

$4\overline{)37}$

A. 11 R4
B. 10 R7
C. 9 R1
D. 8 R5

3. Which solid shape has one flat surface that is a circle?

A. Cylinder   **C.** Sphere
B. Cone   **D.** Pyramid

4. Multiply.

8×6

A. 24   **C.** 42
B. 36   **D.** 48

5. Edna is playing a board game. She needs to move exactly 11 spaces to reach the finish. The game's spinner is marked with the digits 1, 2, 3, and 4. What is the fewest number of spins Edna will need to make to reach the finish?

_____

6. The Great Pyramid of Giza has 4 equal sides that are shaped like huge triangles. How many edges does the pyramid have?

_____

Spiral Review and Test Prep 8-4

Circle the correct answer.

1. A case of eggs contains 144 eggs. Each egg carton holds 12 eggs. How many cartons are in a case of eggs?

   A. 10   **C.** 14
   B. 12   **D.** 16

2. Which solid has the most number of edges?

   A. Cube   **C.** Pyramid
   B. Sphere   **D.** Cylinder

3. $21 \div 3 =$

   A. 7   **C.** 12
   B. 11   **D.** 24

4. Which multiplication sentence is the same as $6 + 6 + 6 + 6 = n$?

   A. $3 \times 6 = n$
   B. $4 \times 6 = n$
   C. $5 \times 6 = n$
   D. $6 \times 6 = n$

5. Karin made a bracelet of beads. For every 3 yellow beads in the bracelet, she used 1 blue bead. Her bracelet has 6 blue beads. Act it out to find out how many beads in total Karin used.

   _____

   _____

6. Brian's class has 3 fish tanks. One tank contains 9 fish, the second has 11 fish, and the third has 13 fish. To make each tank hold the same number of fish, what must Brian do?

   _____

   _____

   _____

   _____

© Pearson Education, Inc. 3

Spiral Review and Test Prep 8-5

Circle the correct answer.

1. Margie wants to grow 3 more rows of beans than carrots. A package of carrot seeds will plant 2 rows. A package of bean seeds will plant 3 rows. If she plants 6 rows of carrots, how many packages of bean seeds does she need?

A. 3   **C.** 5
B. 4   **D.** 6

2. Divide mentally.

$0 \div 5$

A. 0   **C.** 5
B. 1   **D.** 15

3. Which of the following geometric terms best describes a set of railroad tracks?

A. Points
B. Intersecting lines
C. Parallel lines
D. Rays

Solve the problem by acting it out. Write the answer in a complete sentence.

4. Jenny made 5 baskets for every 2 her sister made. If her sister made 6 baskets, how many did Jenny make?

_____

5. List four numbers that are divisible by 10.

_____

_____

6. How many students subscribed to more than three magazines?

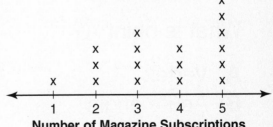

Magazine Sales

Number of Magazine Subscriptions

_____

Spiral Review and Test Prep 8-6

Circle the correct answer.

1. Which number completes this fact family?

$8 \times y = 64 \quad 64 \div y = 8$

A. 9   **C.** 7
B. 8   **D.** 6

2. One box of marbles has 8 red, 6 yellow, and 3 blue marbles. Alex has 2 boxes of marbles. How many more red marbles than blue marbles does he have?

A. 5   **C.** 12
B. 10   **D.** 16

3.

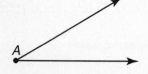

What is point *A*?

A. Vertex
B. Acute angle
C. Obtuse angle
D. Right angle

4. Draw a pair of lines that do not intersect.

5. In the United States, about 58,500,000 dogs are kept as pets by people. There are also about 72,600,000 pet cats in the country. Write an expression to show the difference between the number of dogs and the number of cats that are kept as pets in the United States.

_____

_____

_____

Multiply.

6. 5×7

_____

Spiral Review and Test Prep 8-7

● Circle the correct answer.

1. The slide costs $1. The Ferris wheel costs $2. Bob and Alice went on each ride the same number of times. Together they spent $12. How many times were they on each ride?

   A. 5   **C.** 3
   B. 4   **D.** 2

● **2.** Divide.   **A.** 2 R1
                     B. 2 R2
   9)19   **C.** 3 R1
                     D. 3 R2

3. How many angles are there in this polygon?

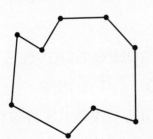

   A. 6   **C.** 8
   B. 7   **D.** 9

4. How can you use multiplication to find 28 ÷ 2?

_____

5. Draw two different obtuse angles.

6. Catherine Ndereba of Kenya set the women's world record for running a marathon race in October 2001. She began running at 6:30 A.M. and crossed the finish line at 9:48 A.M. and 47 sec. For how long did Ndereba run?

_____

_____

Spiral Review and Test Prep 8-8

Circle the correct answer.

1. Which of the following is a multiple of 11?

    A. 13   **C.** 35

    B. 22   **D.** 48

2. There are 17 students in Alisa's class. She wants to bake cupcakes for everyone. Each batch makes 6 cupcakes, and 2 eggs are needed to make a batch. How many eggs will Alisa need altogether?

    A. 4   **C.** 8

    B. 6   **D.** 10

3. Suppose you bought a card that cost $2.78 and paid with a $5 bill. What change should you receive?

    A. $2.22   **C.** $3.02

    B. $2.32   **D.** $3.12

4. Write a multiplication sentence that will help you divide 36 by 9.

_____

_____

5.

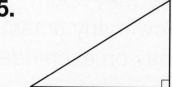

Name the triangle in two different ways.

_____

_____

6.

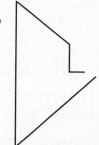

Is the figure above a polygon? If it is a polygon, give its name. If not, explain why.

_____

_____

Spiral Review and Test Prep 8-9

● Circle the correct answer.

1. Divide.

40 ÷ 8

A. 10   **C.** 5
B. 8   **D.** 4

2. A room with four sides measures 90 ft on each side. What is its shape?

A. Triangle
B. Rectangle
C. Trapezoid
D. Square

3. At Hoshi's school, the choices for breakfast cereal are corn flakes, bran flakes, and oatmeal. The cereal can be topped with blueberries, strawberries, or bananas. How many different cereal choices are offered?

A. 15   **C.** 9
B. 12   **D.** 6

4. Kyle has 15 model cars. His friend Zach has 3 times as many cars. Write a numerical expression for the number of cars Zach has.

_____

5. Draw two different isosceles triangles.

Spiral Review and Test Prep 8-10

Circle the correct answer.

1. Which number completes both number sentences?

$$6 \times a = 42 \quad 42 \div a = 6$$

A. 5   **C.** 7
B. 6   **D.** 8

2. A guitar has 6 strings. A violin has 4 strings. In Tim's music school, there are 3 guitars and 4 violins. How many strings do these instruments have altogether?

A. 21   **C.** 28
B. 24   **D.** 34

3. Divide.

$$12\overline{)146}$$

A. 12 R2
B. 140 R6
C. 136 R10
D. 135 R11

4.

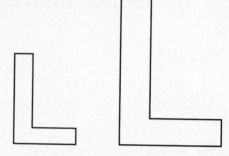

Are the figures congruent? Write *yes* or *no*.

_____

5. Draw a rhombus.

6. Multiply.

$$3 \times 9 = \underline{\qquad}$$

Spiral Review and Test Prep 8-11

● Circle the correct answer.

1. Skip count backward by 5s to solve.

85 ÷ 5 =

A. 15   **C.** 19
B. 17   **D.** 20

2.

A highway "Yield" sign is an isosceles triangle. How many lines of symmetry can you draw in the yield sign?

A. 3   **C.** 1
B. 2   **D.** 0

3. Add.

326 + 243 =

A. 469   **C.** 569
B. 479   **D.** 579

4. Write a division story for 24 ÷ 12 = n.

_____

_____

_____

_____

5.

Did the figure move by a slide, flip, or turn?

_____

6. Tim needs 18 pens. He can buy them in packages of 6, 9, or 12. What kind of packages should he buy? Write two different ways Tim could buy exactly 18 pens.

_____

Spiral Review and Test Prep 8-12

Circle the correct answer.

1. Divide.

$4\overline{)40}$

A. 10
B. 11
C. 12
D. 13

2. 45 ÷ 5

A. 6   C. 8
B. 7   D. 9

3. There are 21 students in one class and 19 in another. The lab has 34 computers. How many students will need to share a computer when both classes are in the lab at the same time?

A. 6   C. 9
B. 7   D. 12

4. A shape has 16 equal sides. Each side is 2 in. long. What is the perimeter?

A. 12 in.   C. 24 in.
B. 16 in.   D. 32 in.

5.

Is the figure symmetric? Write *yes* or *no*.

_____

6.

Favorite Colors

Color	Tally	Count
Red	ℍℍ III	8
Blue	III	3
Green	II	2
Yellow	IIII	4
Orange	ℍℍ	5
Purple	ℍℍ I	6

Which color was the favorite in this survey?

_____

7. How many total votes did red and yellow receive in the survey?

_____

Spiral Review and Test Prep 8-13

Circle the correct answer.

1. Which shows the rule for dividing by 1?

   A. $18 \div 3 = 6$
   B. $18 \div 6 = 3$
   C. $18 \div 1 = 18$
   D. $18 \div 1 = 1$

2.

What is the area of the figure?

   A. 20 square units
   B. 22 square units
   C. 23 square units
   D. 24 square units

3. Multiply.

   $9 \times 8 \times 3 =$

   A. 72   **C.** 216
   B. 206   **D.** 243

4. Write the fact family for 7, 8, and 56.

_____

_____

_____

5. Five children played ring toss at the school fair. Bill went first. Marlene went after Tony. Jill went before Tony. If Jamal went last, who was second?

_____

6.

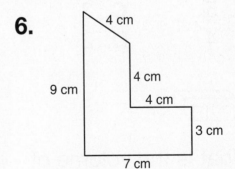

What is the perimeter of the figure?

_____

Name_____

Spiral Review and Test Prep 8-14

Circle the correct answer.

1. What multiplication
   sentence will help you
   solve $33 \div 3$?

   A. $3 \times 6 = 18$
   B. $3 \times 8 = 24$
   C. $3 \times 10 = 30$
   D. $3 \times 11 = 33$

2. There are 14 students in
   music class. They sing
   a song with 30 verses.
   If each sings at least
   2 verses, how many will
   sing 3 verses?

   A. 5   **C.** 3
   B. 4   **D.** 2

3.

   What is the volume of
   the figure?

   A. 2 cubic units
   B. 4 cubic units
   C. 8 cubic units
   D. 16 cubic units

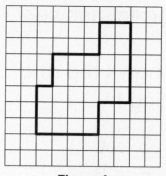

Figure A

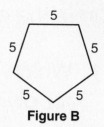

Figure B

4. Does Figure A have the
   same perimeter as
   Figure B? Explain.

   _____

   _____

   _____

   _____

   _____

5. There are 9 shelves and
   27 basketballs. How
   many basketballs are
   on each shelf?

   _____

Spiral Review and Test Prep 8-15

Circle the correct answer.

1. Divide.

$56 \div 7 =$

A. 6   **C.** 8

B. 7   **D.** 9

2. What is the remainder when you divide 93 by 9?

A. 3   **C.** 5

B. 4   **D.** 6

3.

What is the volume of the figure?

A. 12 cubic units

B. 14 cubic units

C. 16 cubic units

D. 18 cubic units

4. The spinner on Mike's board game is marked with the digits 2, 4, 6, and 8. Mike says he can spin three times and get a total of 15 exactly. Is this true? Explain.

_____

_____

_____

_____

5.

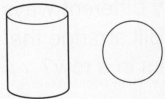

Write a sentence to describe how the figures are alike.

_____

_____

_____

Spiral Review and Test Prep 9-1

Circle the correct answer.

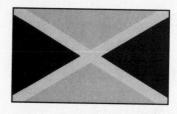

1. Which is NOT the time shown on the clock?

A. 9:42

B. 18 min to ten

C. 8 min to ten

D. 42 min after nine

2. Bill has 4 letter blocks: *A, B, C,* and *D.* How many different ways can Bill arrange the blocks in a row?

A. 6   **C.** 18

B. 12   **D.** 24

3. Which is the difference of 81 − 15?

A. 66   **C.** 56

B. 64   **D.** 55

4. How many triangles in Jamaica's flag are obtuse?

_____

5. How many lines of symmetry does the flag of Jamaica have?

_____

6. How many triangles are on 5 Jamaican flags?

_____

7. Describe how a square pyramid and a cube are alike.

_____

_____

_____

_____

Name_____

Spiral Review and Test Prep 9-2

● Circle the correct answer.

1. Which shape has 4 sides and 4 right angles?

   A. Parallelogram
   B. Trapezoid
   C. Triangle
   D. Rectangle

2. Name the equal parts of the whole.

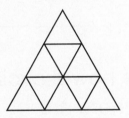

   A. Sixths
   B. Ninths
   C. Sevenths
   D. Eighths

3. Round to estimate the sum of 37 + 26.

   A. 60   **C.** 80
   B. 70   **D.** 90

4.

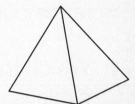

Describe how a pyramid and a triangle are alike.

_____

_____

_____

5.

Draw a right angle on the clock face at 3:00.

6. Each week, Kevin's task is to sweep out the garage. His sister Gail has to take out the trash every third day. How many times do Kevin and Gail each do their tasks over 3 weeks?

_____

Spiral Review and Test Prep 9-3

Circle the correct answer.

1. Which fraction of the circle is shaded?

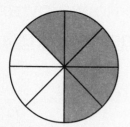

A. $\frac{5}{6}$ **C.** $\frac{5}{8}$

B. $\frac{6}{8}$ **D.** $\frac{5}{9}$

2. Which solid figure is Earth most like?

A. Cylinder
B. Rectangular prism
C. Cone
D. Sphere

3. Which is true of a line segment?

A. Endless in one direction
B. Part of a line
C. Endless in each direction
D. An exact point

4. Find the sum of 638 + 175.

_____

5.

Name the equal parts of the whole.

_____

6. Describe how a circle and a sphere are different.

_____

_____

_____

7. A minivan may weigh 4,628 lb. Write the word form for this number.

_____

Spiral Review and Test Prep 9-4

● Circle the correct answer.

1. Ben cut his peanut butter and jelly sandwich into four equal pieces. He ate one piece. Which is the fraction of the sandwich Ben ate?

A. $\frac{2}{8}$ C. $\frac{1}{2}$

B. $\frac{1}{4}$ D. $\frac{3}{4}$

2. Katie has $17 to spend. If she spends $8, which number sentence tells how much she has left?

A. $17 − $8 = n
B. $18 − $7 = n
C. $17 − $9 = n
D. $18 − $8 = n

3. Which is the product of 9 × 0?

A. 0   C. 9

B. 1   D. 90

4.

Find the volume of the figure.

_____

5. Complete the number sentence.

$$\frac{1}{3} = \frac{\boxed{}}{6}$$

6. Are the balloons congruent?

_____

7. Use geometric terms to describe how a basketball and a baseball are alike.

_____

_____

Name_____

Spiral Review and Test Prep 9-5

Circle the correct answer.

1. The length of a side of a square is 6 units. What is the perimeter?

  A. 6   **C.** 24
  B. 12   **D.** 36

2. Alex is twice as old as Karen is. Karen is 7 years old. How old is Alex?

  A. 9   **C.** 14
  B. 12   **D.** 16

3. Which is the quotient of 5 ÷ 1?

  A. 6   **C.** 2
  B. 5   **D.** 1

4. Which is next in the pattern 36, 30, 24, 18, 12, ▪?

  A. 6   **C.** 1
  B. 4   **D.** 0

5.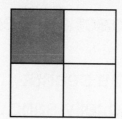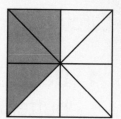

Compare. Write >, <, or =.

$\frac{1}{4}\bigcirc\frac{3}{8}$

6. Complete the number sentence.

$\frac{2}{6}=\frac{\square}{12}$

7. Which polygon has 6 sides?

8. Wendy put 2 marbles in the first circle, 4 marbles in the second circle, and 8 marbles in the third circle. If the pattern continues, how many marbles will be in the sixth circle?

Spiral Review and Test Prep 9-6

Circle the correct answer.

1. Estimate the amount that is shaded.

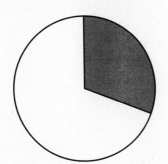

A. $\frac{1}{6}$ **C.** $\frac{1}{2}$

B. $\frac{1}{3}$ **D.** $\frac{2}{3}$

2. Find the perimeter.

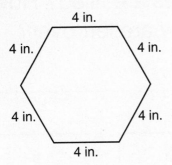

4 in.
4 in.   4 in.
4 in.   4 in.
4 in.

A. 16 in.   **C.** 24 in.
B. 20 in.   **D.** 28 in.

3. Which type of angle is less than 90°?

A. Obtuse   **C.** Right
B. Acute   **D.** Straight

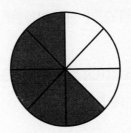

4.

Compare. Write >, <, or =.

$\frac{5}{8}$ ◯ $\frac{4}{5}$

5. Solve by acting it out. Write the answer in a complete sentence.

In softball, a runner touches 4 bases each time she scores. How many bases does a runner touch if she scores 5 runs?

6. Ann, Katie, and Michelle are going to share 9 dolls equally. How many

Spiral Review and Test Prep 9-7

Circle the correct answer.

1. Which fraction is missing on the number line?

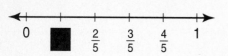

A. $\frac{1}{5}$ **C.** $\frac{2}{4}$

B. $\frac{2}{5}$ **D.** $\frac{2}{3}$

2. Which angle is greater than a right angle?

A. Obtuse angle
B. Acute angle
C. Right angle
D. 75° angle

3. Which is the name of this quadrilateral?

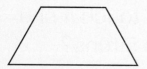

A. Rectangle
B. Rhombus
C. Trapezoid
D. Parallelogram

4. Estimate the amount that is left.

_____

5. Dylan is putting 17 glasses into boxes. Each box will hold 6 glasses. How many boxes are filled? How many are left over?

_____

6.

Describe how Quadrilateral A and Quadrilateral B are alike.

_____

_____

_____

Spiral Review and Test Prep 9-8

Circle the correct answer.

1. There are 23 dogs. Three are poodles, 16 are huskies, and 4 are terriers. What fraction of the dogs are poodles?

A. $\frac{2}{23}$ **C.** $\frac{4}{23}$

B. $\frac{3}{23}$ **D.** $\frac{16}{23}$

2. Which statement is true about parallelograms?

A. They have 4 right angles.
B. There is only one pair of parallel sides.
C. They have 1 90° angle.
D. Opposite sides are parallel.

3. Which figure has 6 faces?

A. Pyramid
B. Sphere
C. Cone
D. Cube

4. Write the missing fractions of the number line.

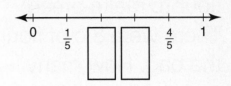

5. Find 26 + 9.

_____

6. Harry and his brother Pete are riding their bicycles around a track. For every 2 laps Harry finishes, Pete finishes 3 laps. How many laps does Harry finish if Pete finishes 9 laps?

_____

_____

_____

_____

Spiral Review and Test Prep 9-9

Circle the correct answer.

1. Alex used $\frac{1}{4}$ of a bag of flour to make bread. There were 8 c of flour in the bag. How many cups of flour did he use?

   A. 4   **C.** 2
   B. 3   **D.** 1

2. Which solid figure does an apple most look like?

   A. Cone
   B. Cube
   C. Rectangular prism
   D. Sphere

3. How many sides does this polygon have?

   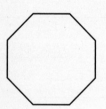

   A. 10   **C.** 8
   B. 9   **D.** 6

4. Five boys and 5 girls sing in a choir. What fraction of the choir members are boys?

   _____

5. At how many points do intersecting lines cross?

   _____

6.

   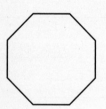

   Describe how Figure A and Figure B are alike.

   _____

   _____

   _____

7. Add.

   $156 + 235 =$

   _____

Name_____

Spiral Review and Test Prep 9-10

Circle the correct answer.

1. Add.

$$\frac{3}{7} + \frac{2}{7} =$$

A. $\frac{6}{7}$ **C.** $\frac{4}{7}$

B. $\frac{5}{7}$ **D.** $\frac{1}{7}$

2. How many lines of symmetry does the figure have?

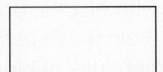

A. 1   **C.** 3

B. 2   **D.** 4

3. One half of the students in a class are girls. There are 24 students in the class. How many students are girls?

A. 8   **C.** 14

B. 12   **D.** 18

4. Which point is located at (4, 6)?

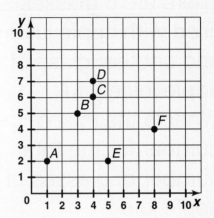

5. What is the name of the triangle with three equal sides?

6. I am a cube. My friend has the same number of edges and faces as I do. Not all of my friend's faces are the same shape. What kind of solid figure is my friend?

Spiral Review and Test Prep 9-11

Circle the correct answer.

1. There are 5 glasses filled with apple juice and another glass of apple juice $\frac{3}{4}$ full. What is the mixed number for the total number of glasses of apple juice?

   A. $4\frac{1}{4}$ **C.** $5\frac{1}{2}$

   B. $5\frac{1}{4}$ **D.** $5\frac{3}{4}$

2. Find the area of a postcard with a length of 4 in. and a width of 6 in.

   A. 48 in.^{2} **C.** 20 in.^{2}

   B. 24 in.^{2} **D.** 12 in.^{2}

3. How are the figures related?

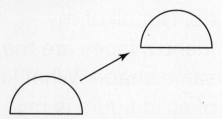

   A. Slide   **C.** Turn

   B. Flip   **D.** Slip

4. Add.

$$\frac{4}{8} + \frac{3}{8} =$$

_____

5. Subtract.

$$\frac{5}{7} - \frac{2}{7} =$$

_____

6. Yvonne is building a town with blocks. She used 3 blocks to build the first house, 4 blocks to build the second house, and 5 blocks to build the third house. If the pattern continues, how many blocks will Yvonne use for the eighth house?

_____

Spiral Review and Test Prep 9-12

Circle the correct answer.

1. How many parallelograms are in the figure?

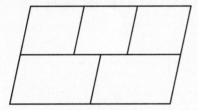

A. 15   **C.** 6
B. 10   **D.** 5

2. Which is NOT a multiple of 9?

A. 18   **C.** 84
B. 72   **D.** 99

3. There are 6 bottles of water and $\frac{1}{2}$ of another bottle of water. What is the mixed number for the total number of bottles of water?

A. $5\frac{1}{2}$ **C.** $6\frac{1}{2}$
B. $6\frac{1}{4}$ **D.** $7\frac{1}{2}$

4. What is the area of a square with a side of 5 units?

_____

5. Can two lines be parallel? How?

_____

_____

_____

_____

6.

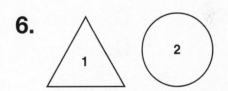

Describe how Figure 1 and Figure 2 are different.

_____

_____

_____

_____

Name_____

Spiral Review and Test Prep 9-13

Circle the correct answer.

1. How long is the bookmark to the nearest inch?

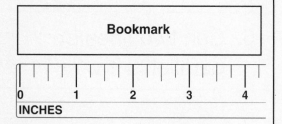

Bookmark

INCHES

  A. 5 in.   **C.** 4 in.
  B. $4\frac{1}{2}$ in.   **D.** 3 in.

2. Compare.

69 + 18 ⬤ 87

  A. >   **C.** =
  B. <   **D.** +

3. Which is NOT equal to 896?

  A. 8 hundreds 9 tens 6 ones

  B. 7 hundreds 19 tens 6 ones

  C. 7 hundreds 9 tens 6 ones

  D. 8 hundred 8 tens 16 ones

4. Kathy had an orange. She cut it in half and then she cut each piece in half again. She ate 3 pieces. What fraction of the orange is left?

_____

5. The flag of Panama has 1 red star and 1 blue star. How many stars are there on 6 flags of Panama?

_____

6. Name a solid figure with five flat surfaces.

_____

7. Are two pennies congruent?

_____

Name_____

Spiral Review and Test Prep 9-14

● Circle the correct answer.

1. How long is the candle to the nearest inch?

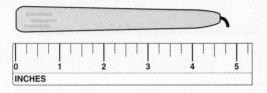

A. 6 in.   **C.** 4 in.
B. 5 in.   **D.** 3 in.

2. How long is the paperclip to the nearest $\frac{1}{4}$ in.?

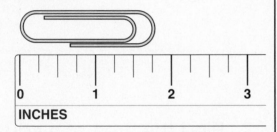

A. 1 in.   **C.** $1\frac{3}{4}$ in.
B. $1\frac{1}{2}$ in.   **D.** 2 in.

3. Sherry has 12 crayons to share equally with Linda and Ellen. How many will they each get?

A. 2   **C.** 4
B. 3   **D.** 12

4. How many faces does a pyramid have?

_____

5. Find the perimeter of a rectangle with a length of 11 ft and a width of 4 ft.

_____

6. Describe how a cone and a cylinder are alike.

_____

_____

_____

_____

_____

_____

Spiral Review and Test Prep 9-15

Circle the correct answer.

1. How many inches are in 3 ft?

   A. 12 in.   **C.** 36 in.
   B. 24 in.   **D.** 48 in.

2. There are a total of 15 buttons on 3 identical shirts. How many buttons are on each shirt?

   A. 5   **C.** 3
   B. 4   **D.** 2

3. Round 842 to the nearest ten.

   A. 850   **C.** 840
   B. 842   **D.** 800

4. Add.

   $128 + 331 + 15 =$

   A. 384   **C.** 484
   B. 474   **D.** 487

5. Measure the line segment to the nearest $\frac{1}{2}$ in.

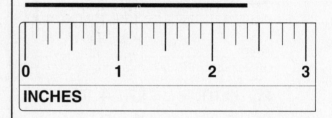

_____

6. What is the name of a triangle with 3 equal sides and 3 acute angles?

_____

7. Find the area of a square with a side of 3 ft.

_____

8. Josh is 7 times as old as Steve. Steve is 3 years old. How old is Josh?

_____

Spiral Review and Test Prep 9-16

Circle the correct answer.

1. How many feet are there in 2 yd?

   A. 12 ft   **C.** 6 ft
   B. 8 ft   **D.** 4 ft

2. There are 6 squares on each cube. How many squares are there in 3 cubes?

   A. 12   **C.** 18
   B. 16   **D.** 24

3. How many inches are in $\frac{1}{3}$ ft?

   A. 2 in.   **C.** 4 in.
   B. 3 in.   **D.** 6 in.

4. Use mental math to find the sum of $15 + 37$.

   A. 53   **C.** 43
   B. 52   **D.** 42

5. Find the volume of a cube with an edge of 4 ft.

_____

6. Find the product of 0×8.

_____

7. Sarah has $\frac{1}{3}$ as many books as Mark does. Mark has 15 books. How many books does Sarah have? Write your answer in a complete sentence.

_____

_____

_____

8. How many inches are in 2 yd?

_____

Spiral Review and Test Prep 9-17

Circle the correct answer.

1. There are 16 people at a party. A whole pizza costs $9 and can be cut into 8 slices. How many pizzas are needed for each person to get exactly one slice of pizza?

   A. 2   **C.** 6
   B. 4   **D.** 8

2. Which is the product of 8 × 5?

   A. 25   **C.** 40
   B. 35   **D.** 65

3. Round 687 to the nearest ten.

   A. 600   **C.** 690
   B. 680   **D.** 700

4. How many sides does a pentagon have?

   A. 8   **C.** 5
   B. 6   **D.** 4

5. How many feet are in 4 yd?

   _____

6. Find the area of a 6 in. square picture frame.

   _____

7. Find the product of 5 × 6 × 2.

   _____

8. Describe how the two triangles are alike.

   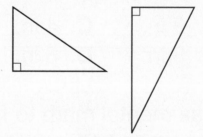

   _____

   _____

Spiral Review and Test Prep 10-1

● Circle the correct answer.

1. Frank sold several scented candles and 9 unscented candles. The scented candles cost $15 each and the unscented candles cost $12 each. How much money did Frank collect for the scented candles?

   A. $60
   B. $75
   C. $108
   D. Missing information

2. Which is the product of 6 × 8?

   A. 40   **C.** 56
   B. 48   **D.** 72

3. How many feet are in a mile?

   A. 5,280   **C.** 5,600
   B. 5,500   **D.** 5,720

Add or subtract. You may use fraction strips or draw pictures to help.

4. $\frac{1}{8} + \frac{3}{8} =$ _____

5. $\frac{9}{10} - \frac{2}{10} =$ _____

6. Julia has 7 key chains from different countries, 21 key chains from different states in the U.S., and 28 key chains from different businesses. What fraction of key chains does she have from different countries?

   _____

7. Harry made 6 beaded bracelets. He gave 3 to his mother. Then he divided the rest between 3 friends. How many bracelets did each friend get?

   _____

Spiral Review and Test Prep 10-2

Circle the correct answer.

1. Brandon is 10 years old. He is 4 ft 9 in. tall. How tall is Brandon in inches?

   A. 48   **C.** 58
   B. 57   **D.** 59

2. How many yards are in 1 mi?

   A. 15,432   **C.** 3,496
   B. 5,280   **D.** 1,760

3. Which fraction is the same as the decimal 0.3?

   A. $\frac{3}{100}$ **C.** $\frac{3}{10}$
   B. $\frac{1}{10}$ **D.** $\frac{3}{5}$

4. Add.

   $71 + 52 + 147 =$

   A. 199   **C.** 270
   B. 269   **D.** 271

Decide if the problem has extra information or missing information. Solve if you have enough information.

5. Tim earns $3 each time he walks Mr. McCarthy's dog. Tim usually walks the dog after school. How much did Tim earn last week?

   _____

6. Kendra had a sandwich. She cut it in fourths, then she cut each piece in half. She ate 2 pieces of the sandwich. How many pieces did she have left?

   _____

7. Subtract.

   $376 - 187 =$ _____

Spiral Review and Test Prep 10-3

Circle the correct answer.

1. Round to the nearest ten to estimate the sum of 59 and 24.

A. 60   **C.** 80
B. 70   **D.** 90

2. Which is the decimal for $\frac{27}{100}$?

A. 0.3   **C.** 0.72
B. 0.27   **D.** 2.27

3. Which figure is NOT a polygon?

A. Triangle
B. Circle
C. Square
D. Rectangle

4. Write $\frac{7}{10}$ as a decimal.

_____

5. $\frac{1}{4} = \frac{\square}{12}$

6. Order the fractions from least to greatest.

$$\frac{1}{3}, \frac{1}{2}, \frac{1}{10}, \frac{1}{5}$$

_____

Decide if the problem has extra information or missing information. Solve if you have enough information.

7. Neil bought 3 packs of cards. Each pack had 8 cards. Tina bought 2 packs. How many cards did Neil buy altogether?

_____

_____

Spiral Review and Test Prep 10-4

Circle the correct answer.

1. Which value for x makes $\frac{2}{10} = \frac{x}{5}$ true?

   A. 4   **C.** 2
   B. 3   **D.** 1

2. Which is the next number in the pattern?

   40, 35, 30, 25, ▨

   A. 25   **C.** 15
   B. 20   **D.** 10

3. Subtract.

   $208 - 139 =$

   A. 59
   B. 68
   C. 69
   D. 71

4. Martha makes quilts. She has 3 yd of blue fabric, 8 yd of red fabric, and 1 yd of white fabric. What fraction of the fabric is blue?

   A. $\frac{2}{12}$ **C.** $\frac{4}{12}$
   B. $\frac{3}{12}$ **D.** $\frac{5}{12}$

5. Compare. Use $<$, $>$, or $=$.

   0.36 ◯ 0.73

6. Use the fact $9 + 7 = 16$ to find $16 - 7 =$ _____.

7. Write the fraction for 65 hundredths.

   _____

Solve. Write the answer in a complete sentence.

8. How many squares are in the figure?

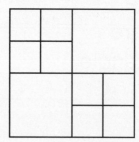

   _____

   _____

   _____

Spiral Review and Test Prep 10-5

Circle the correct answer.

1. Subtract.

$5.57 - 3.67 =$

A. 1.90   **C.** 2.10

B. 2.00   **D.** 2.90

2. Mitzi's dog, Indiana, is 17 months old. How old is Indiana in years?

A. $1\frac{1}{12}$ years old

B. $1\frac{5}{12}$ years old

C. $1\frac{7}{12}$ years old

D. 2 years old

3. How many inches is 2 ft 4 in.?

A. 28   **C.** 20

B. 24   **D.** 18

4. Order the numbers from greatest to least.

0.05, 0.32, 0.18, 0.44, 0.5

_____

_____

5. Compare. Use $>$, $<$, or $=$.

$\frac{6}{7}$ ◯ $\frac{5}{7}$

Decide if the problem has extra information or missing information. Solve if you have enough information.

6. Town A has 8 fire engines. Town B has 5 fire engines. Town C has 9 fire engines. How many more fire engines does Town A have than Town B?

_____

_____

Spiral Review and Test Prep 10-6

Circle the correct answer.

1. Add.

$$150 + 225 + 889 =$$

A. 1,265   **C.** 1,263
B. 1,264   **D.** 1,164

2. In a math class there are 2 students who want to be doctors, 18 students who want to be engineers, 17 students who want to be computer programmers, and 4 students who want to be mathematicians. What fraction of the students want to be engineers?

A. $\frac{17}{41}$ **C.** $\frac{17}{40}$

B. $\frac{18}{41}$ **D.** $\frac{18}{40}$

3. Which is the product of 3×9?

A. 37   **C.** 27
B. 30   **D.** 18

4. How many ways can you write the numbers 1, 2, and 3 in a different order? Continue the list to find all the ways.

123, 132, 213,

_____

_____

5. Add.

$$2.39 + 4.73 = \underline{\hspace{1cm}}$$

6. Add.

$$\frac{2}{6} + \frac{3}{6} = \underline{\hspace{1cm}}$$

7. Laszlo Biro invented the ballpoint pen. In 2002, about 20,000,000 ballpoint pens were sold every day. The year 2002 is 64 years after Mr. Biro invented the pen. In what year did he invent it?

_____

Name _____

Spiral Review and Test Prep 10-7

● Circle the correct answer.

1. Which fraction is to the right of $\frac{1}{2}$ on a number line?

A. $\frac{1}{4}$ **C.** $\frac{1}{5}$

B. $\frac{1}{3}$ **D.** $\frac{2}{3}$

2. A decimeter is how many centimeters?

A. 1,000   **C.** 10
B. 100   **D.** 1

3. Find the sum using mental math.

64 + 18 =

A. 92   **C.** 82
B. 88   **D.** 80

4. Multiply.

$4 \times 7 \times 2 =$

A. 56   **C.** 28
B. 54   **D.** 14

5. In how many ways can you choose two colors from red, white, blue, and green? Continue the list to find all the ways.

Red/white, red/blue, red/green, white/blue,

_____

6. Complete the number sentence.

$\frac{4}{20} = \dfrac{\boxed{}}{5}$

7. Compare. Use $<$, $>$, or $=$.

$\frac{1}{5} \bigcirc \frac{3}{15}$

8. Hayley lined up with 5 other students. Ned is third in line. Mike is right behind Hayley. Betty is ahead of Ned. If Wendi is first in line, who is last?

Spiral Review and Test Prep 10-8

Circle the correct answer.

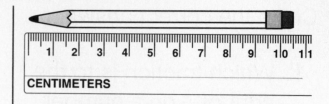

CENTIMETERS

1. How many centimeters are in 1 m?

   A. 1,000   **C.** 20
   B. 100   **D.** 10

2. Which statement about quadrilaterals is NOT true?

   A. A square is a kind of rectangle.
   B. A rectangle is a kind of parallelogram.
   C. A trapezoid is a kind of quadrilateral.
   D. A rhombus is a kind of trapezoid.

3. How many yards are equal to 72 in.?

   A. 8   **C.** 4
   B. 6   **D.** 2

4. Measure the pencil to the nearest centimeter.

   _____

5. How many inches are equal to 2 ft 3 in.?

   _____

Decide if the problem has extra information or missing information. Solve if you have enough information.

6. For each newspaper Uma delivers, she receives $0.25. Uma delivers newspapers 3 times each week. How much money does she earn?

   _____

Name_____

Spiral Review and Test Prep 10-9

Circle the correct answer.

1. Which solid figure does a ball look like?

   A. Sphere

   B. Cube

   C. Rectangular prism

   D. Cone

2. Sam is 3 years older than John. Clayton is 3 years old and John is 4 years old. How old is Sam?

   A. 6   **C.** 8

   B. 7   **D.** 9

3. Sandra cut a peach in half. Then she cut each half into thirds. She ate 2 pieces. What fraction of the peach is left?

   A. $\frac{1}{5}$ **C.** $\frac{2}{6}$

   B. $\frac{1}{3}$ **D.** $\frac{4}{6}$

4. Name an object that is about 10 cm long. Explain why you think the object is about 10 cm long.

_____

_____

_____

_____

_____

5. How many meters are in 1 km?

_____

6. Write a mixed number for the picture.

_____

Spiral Review and Test Prep 11-1

Circle the correct answer.

1. Which is the best estimate for the height of a flagpole?

   A. 10 mm   C. 10 m
   B. 10 cm   D. 10 km

2. Which is the greatest?

   A. 615   C. 547
   B. 123   D. 229

3. Which is the least?

   A. 1,823   C. 2,010
   B. 1,213   D. 1,923

4. Brianne is buying a name tag for her dog's collar. It can be made in one of 6 colors, and in one of 2 shapes. How many different tags can Brianne chose?

   A. 2   C. 8
   B. 6   D. 12

5. There are 10 waffles in a box. Glen ate 3 of them. Write a decimal to show how much of the waffles he ate.

   _____

6. Explain how to measure the length of the snake.

   _____

   _____

   _____

   _____

   _____

   _____

   _____

Spiral Review and Test Prep 11-2

Circle the correct answer.

1. Add.

   $23 + 68 =$

   A. 81   **C.** 91
   B. 85   **D.** 101

2. Which is the sum of
   $54 + 36$?

   A. 80   **C.** 96
   B. 90   **D.** 100

3. What decimal names
   the same amount as
   $\frac{61}{100}$?

   A. 6.1   **C.** 0.16
   B. 0.61   **D.** 0.06

4. What decimal names
   the same amount as
   four tenths?

   A. 40.0   **C.** 0.4
   B. 4.0   **D.** 0.04

5. A bathtub can hold
   50 gal of water. How
   many gallons of water
   will 6 bathtubs hold?

   _____

6. Explain how the number
   of sprouts changes as
   the number of days
   changes.

Days	1	2	3	4
Sprouts	1	16	32	48

   _____

   _____

   _____

   _____

   _____

   _____

Spiral Review and Test Prep 11-3

Circle the correct answer.

1. Which is the missing number in 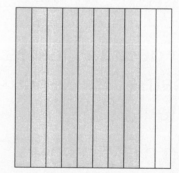 × 8 = 2,400?

  A. 3   **C.** 60

  B. 30   **D.** 300

2. Which is the best estimate for 3 × 189?

  A. 300   **C.** 600

  B. 400   **D.** 900

3. Which unit would you most likely use to measure the width of a street?

  A. Centimeter

  B. Dekameter

  C. Meter

  D. Kilometer

4. Caroline's restaurant has a $2.99 lunch special for a sandwich, a side dish, and a drink. How many different lunch combinations can you buy for $2.99?

LUNCH

Sandwich	Side Dish	Beverage
Roast Beef	Salad	Ice Tea
Fish	Baked Potato	Milk
Veggie Burger	Greens	Juice

5. Write a fraction and a decimal for the shaded part.

Spiral Review and Test Prep 11-4

Circle the correct answer.

1.

96 oz

How is the number shown used?

A. To locate

B. To name

C. To measure

D. To count

2. Multiply.

$8 \times 7 =$

A. 42   **C.** 56

B. 48   **D.** 58

3. Which is the quotient of 6,300 ÷ 7?

A. 80   **C.** 800

B. 90   **D.** 900

Estimate the length of the bandage. Then measure to the nearest centimeter.

4.

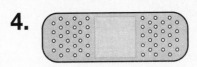

_____

5. Estimate the product of 8 × 482.

_____

6. Three coins are tossed. How many different combinations of heads and tails are possible as the result?

_____

7. Write $\frac{23}{100}$ as a decimal.

_____

Spiral Review and Test Prep 11-5

Circle the correct answer.

1. What fraction of the square is shaded?

A. $\frac{1}{2}$ **C.** $\frac{1}{4}$

B. $\frac{1}{3}$ **D.** $\frac{3}{4}$

2. The beads are colored red, green, blue, and yellow. How many ways can the beads be arranged on a string?

A. 8   **C.** 16

B. 12   **D.** 24

3. Which is the best estimate for the length of a shoe?

A. 15 cm   **C.** 105 cm

B. 35 dm   **D.** 205 dm

4. Add.

$2.54 + 4.91 =$

_____

Use patterns to find each quotient.

5. $48 \div 6 =$ _____

$480 \div 6 =$ _____

$4,800 \div 6 =$ _____

6. A standard-sized brick is 8 in. long. About how many bricks long is a 58 in. wall?

_____

_____

Complete the patterns.

7. 3, 6, 9, ____, ____, ____

8. 124, 118, 112, ____,

____, ____

Spiral Review and Test Prep 11-6

● Circle the correct answer.

1. How many meters are in 1 km?

    A. 10   **C.** 1,000

    B. 100   **D.** 10,000

2. How many diagonals can be drawn in a pentagon?

    A. 12   **C.** 6

    B. 10   **D.** 5

● **3.** Find the elapsed time.

P.M.   P.M.

    A. 3 hr

    B. 3 hr 15 min

    C. 3 hr 45 min

    D. 4 hr 15 min

4. Estimate the quotient of 19 ÷ 4.

_____

5. Draw an array for 3 × 11. Find the product.

6. Compare. Use <, >, or =.

    0.27 ◯ 0.72

7. Frog A leapt 0.485 cm. Frog B leapt 0.51 cm. Which frog leapt farther?

_____

Spiral Review and Test Prep 11-7

Circle the correct answer.

1. Add.

$36 + 58 =$

A. 84   **C.** 94
B. 92   **D.** 96

2. Which is $\frac{43}{100}$ as a decimal?

A. 4.3   **C.** 0.34
B. 0.43   **D.** 0.043

3. Subtract.

$639 - 274 =$

A. 365   **C.** 465
B. 375   **D.** 475

4. Which decimal is greatest?

A. 0.56   **C.** 0.65
B. 0.71   **D.** 0.73

5. Find the product of 4×31.

_____

6. Find the product.

$56 \times 6 =$

_____

7. Matilda is going to the library, the post office, and the grocery store. Make an organized list to show her choices of what order she can go to each place.

_____

_____

_____

8. Find the elapsed time.
Start time: 8:15 A.M.
End time: 2:30 P.M.

_____

© Pearson Education, Inc. 3

Spiral Review and Test Prep 11-8

Circle the correct answer.

1. Which is the product of 3 × 43?

    A. 129   **C.** 111
    B. 119   **D.** 99

2. Find the elapsed time.
Start time: 1:35 A.M.
End time: 9:15 A.M.

    A. 7 hr 40 min
    B. 8 hr
    C. 8 hr 20 min
    D. 8 hr 40 min

3. Multiply.

    62 × 9 =

    A. 448   **C.** 558
    B. 548   **D.** 658

4. Which decimal shows $\frac{64}{100}$?

    A. 64.0   **C.** 0.64
    B. 6.4   **D.** 0.064

Order the decimals from least to greatest.

5. 0.51   0.05   0.6   0.15

_____

6. 0.2   0.02   0.21   0.12

_____

7. In how many orders can four ribbons in the colors blue, green, orange, and red be tied to the tail of a kite?

_____

8. How are the figures related? Write *flip*, *slide*, or *turn*.

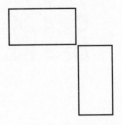

_____

Spiral Review and Test Prep 11-9

Circle the correct answer.

1. Round to the nearest hundred to estimate the sum of 112 + 281.

   A. 300 C. 400
   B. 390 D. 500

2. Which is the product of 349 × 4?

   A. 698   C. 1,298
   B. 896   D. 1,396

3. Add.

   6.4 + 3.9 =

   A. 9.3   C. 10.1
   B. 9.6   D. 10.3

4. Which is the sum of 1.17 + 2.97?

   A. 3.14   C. 4.24
   B. 4.14   D. 4.84

5. Ricky is planting a peach tree, an apple tree, and an orange tree in a row. Make a list to find how many ways the trees can be arranged.

   _____

   _____

Describe the triangle by its sides and its angles.

6.

   _____

7. A storage unit is made of 5 shelves. Each shelf will hold 35 videos. How many videos will the unit hold?

   _____

   _____

Spiral Review and Test Prep 11-10

Circle the correct answer.

1. Which is 87 rounded to the nearest ten?

A. 70   **C.** 90

B. 80   **D.** 100

2. An equilateral triangle has a side length of 427 cm. How many centimeters is its perimeter?

A. 1,281 cm

B. 1,178 cm

C. 854 cm

D. 427 cm

3. Which is the product of $1.47 × 6?

A. $6.42   **C.** $8.82

B. $6.82   **D.** $8.96

4. Add.

$$\frac{6}{8} + \frac{1}{8} =$$

A. $\frac{5}{16}$ **C.** $\frac{7}{16}$

B. $\frac{5}{8}$ **D.** $\frac{7}{8}$

Compare. Use <, >, or =.

5. 0.60 _____ 0.6

6. 1.46 _____ 1.04

7. Mitzi wanted to know how many different sandwiches she could make using the meats bologna, salami, and ham and the cheeses Swiss, American, and cheddar. Each sandwich has one meat and one cheese. Did she find the correct solution? Explain.

Bologna–Swiss	Salami–Swiss	Ham–Swiss
Bologna–American	Salami–American	Ham–American
Bologna–Cheddar	Salami–Cheddar	Ham–Cheddar
	9 different sandwiches	

_____

_____

_____

_____

_____

Spiral Review and Test Prep 11-11

Circle the correct answer.

1. Subtract.

   5.28 − 1.04 =

   A. 424   **C.** 4.24
   B. 6.32   **D.** 3.84

2. Which is the difference of 1.61 − 0.32?

   A. 1.29   **C.** 2.19
   B. 1.93   **D.** 122

3. How many dimes have the same total value as 6 quarters?

   A. 5   **C.** 10
   B. 6   **D.** 15

4. What is the value of one $1 bill, 3 quarters, 1 dime, 1 nickel, and 2 pennies?

   A. $1.67   **C.** $2.02
   B. $1.92   **D.** $2.17

5. One gallon of gasoline cost $1.21. How much did 5 gal of gasoline cost?

   _____

6. Find the product. Estimate to check reasonableness.

   $4.32 × 3

   _____

Write to explain.

7. Tell what part of the whole is shaded. Use tenths and hundredths in your explanation.

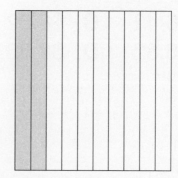

   _____

Name_____

Spiral Review and Test Prep 11-12

Circle the correct answer.

1. Which decimal is greatest?

   A. 0.1   **C.** 0.17
   B. 0.36   **D.** 0.29

2. Which decimal is least?

   A. 0.91   **C.** 0.09
   B. 0.73   **D.** 0.10

3. Mr. Cox needs 2 students to volunteer for an activity. If 8 students volunteer, how many combinations of students could be chosen by Mr. Cox?

   A. 32   **C.** 26
   B. 28   **D.** 18

4. Find $319 × 8 using any computation method.

   A. 2,552   **C.** 2,662
   B. 2,654   **D.** 2,674

5. Four marathon runners are wearing blue, green, red, and white shirts. Their numbers are 3, 17, 24, and 32. Complete the table to find which number matches the green shirt.

- The runner with the lowest number is wearing red.

- Number 17 is not wearing white.

- The runner in green is NOT Number 17 or 32.

	3	17	24	32
blue				
green				
red				
white				

_____

Spiral Review and Test Prep 11-13

Circle the correct answer.

1. Which is the best estimate for the length of a dog's paw?

A. 5 cm   **C.** 5 m

B. 5 dm   **D.** 5 km

2. Which is the best estimate for the length of a dining room?

A. 8 cm   **C.** 8 m

B. 8 dm   **D.** 8 km

3. Which is the quotient of 45 ÷ 5?

A. 3   **C.** 7

B. 6   **D.** 9

4. How many diagonals can be drawn in a square?

A. 0   **C.** 4

B. 2   **D.** 6

5. Find the quotient of 57 ÷ 3.

_____

6. Bob and Cam live in the same apartment building. Each apartment has a three-digit number that begins with the floor that the apartment is on. What is each person's apartment number?

- Bob lives on the second floor; Cam lives one floor above him.
- Both numbers are odd and have zeros in the middle.
- The sum of the ones digits in the two numbers is 4.
- Neither number uses the same digit more than once.

_____

© Pearson Education, Inc. 3

Spiral Review and Test Prep 11-14

Circle the correct answer.

1. How many sides does a pentagon have?

A. 3   **C.** 5

B. 4   **D.** 6

2. Measure to the nearest centimeter.

A. 4 cm   **C.** 6 cm

B. 5 cm   **D.** 7 cm

3. Which is the decimal for $2\frac{1}{10}$?

A. 21.0   **C.** 1.2

B. 2.1   **D.** 0.12

4. Which is the mixed number for 3.3?

A. $3\frac{1}{10}$ **C.** $3\frac{30}{10}$

B. $3\frac{3}{10}$ **D.** $33\frac{1}{10}$

5. Mary and Tom are running for president of the student council. Mason and Lori are running for vice president. How many combinations of president and vice president are possible?

_____

6. Use the break apart method to find the quotient.

$84 \div 4 =$ _____

7. Use place-value blocks or draw a picture to find the quotient.

$38 \div 2 =$ _____

Find each missing number.

8. $8 + 7 =$ _____ $+ 8$

9. _____ $+ 0 = 19$

Spiral Review and Test Prep 11-15

Circle the correct answer.

1. There are 27 students in 3 lines. Each line has the same number of students. How many students are in each line?

   A. 7   **C.** 9

   B. 8   **D.** 10

2. Which is the quotient of $91 \div 4$?

   A. 21 R7   **C.** 22 R3

   B. 22 R1   **D.** 23 R1

3. Use the break apart method to find the quotient.
$48 \div 3$

   A. 24   **C.** 16

   B. 18   **D.** 14

Tell if you would use meters or kilometers for each.

4. the length of a car

_____

5. the distance between two countries

_____

6. Jacob is organizing his model cars. He wants to line up his yellow, red, blue, and green model cars on a shelf. In how many different ways can he line up the model cars?

_____

7. Order $\frac{3}{6}$, $\frac{1}{3}$, and $\frac{1}{8}$ from least to greatest.

_____

Spiral Review and Test Prep 11-16

Circle the correct answer.

1. Which is the decimal for 32 hundredths?

   A. 3,200   **C.** 0.32
   B. 32   **D.** 0.032

2. Which is the difference of 3.45 − 1.77?

   A. 1.58   **C.** 1.68
   B. 1.61   **D.** 5.22

3. What time will you most likely be eating lunch?

   A. 8:30 A.M.
   B. 11:45 A.M.
   C. 3:15 P.M.
   D. 9:07 P.M.

4. It takes 6 c of flour to make a loaf of bread. How many loaves of bread will 81 c of flour make?

   A. 11   **C.** 13
   B. 12   **D.** 14

5. Divide.

   $74 \div 6 =$ _____

6. The triangles shown are made of toothpicks. If the pattern continues, how many toothpicks will be needed to make 7 triangles? Explain how you found your answer.

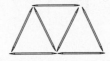

_____

_____

_____

_____

_____

Spiral Review and Test Prep 12-1

Circle the correct answer.

1. Use mental math to find the product of $8 \times 1{,}000$.

   A. 400   **C.** 4,000

   B. 800   **D.** 8,000

2. Which is the product of 6×100?

   A. 30   **C.** 600

   B. 60   **D.** 1,200

3. Which is $1\frac{37}{100}$ as a decimal?

   A. 0.37   **C.** 1.37

   B. 0.137   **D.** 13.7

4. Which is the quotient of $74 \div 8$?

   A. 8   **C.** 9

   B. 8 R10   **D.** 9 R2

Order the fractions from least to greatest.

5. $\frac{2}{3}, \frac{5}{6}, \frac{1}{8}, \frac{4}{7}$

   _____

6. It takes Joel 4 min to read a page of his book. If Joel reads for 91 min, how many full pages will he read?

   _____

7. Bob, Angie, and Liz are in the lunch line. Liz is directly in front of Angie. Bob is not last in line. What order are they in from front to back?

   _____

   _____

   _____

Spiral Review and Test Prep 12-2

Circle the correct answer.

1. How many pints are in 1 gal?

A. 4   **C.** 8
B. 6   **D.** 12

2. Which is the product of 22 × 7?

A. 134   **C.** 144
B. 140   **D.** 154

3. What is the name of the solid figure?

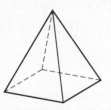

A. Cone   **C.** Sphere
B. Cube   **D.** Pyramid

4. 12 ÷ 3 = _____

120 ÷ 3 = _____

1,200 ÷ 3 = _____

5. A canning jar holds 8 c of sauce. Marie's mother made 62 c of sauce.

  a. How many full jars of sauce will she have?

_____

  b. How many more cups of sauce are needed to fill one more jar?

_____

6. I am a three-digit number that is even. My first and last digits are the same and add up to 8. My middle digit is half of my first digit. What number am I?

_____

Spiral Review and Test Prep 12-3

Circle the correct answer.

1. Which has the greatest capacity?

   A. 1 gal   **C.** 6 pt
   B. 5 qt   **D.** 8 c

2. How many milliliters are in 2 L?

   A. 0.2   **C.** 200
   B. 20   **D.** 2,000

For 3 and 4, find the missing numbers.

3. ■ $\div 5 = 140$

   A. 7   **C.** 90
   B. 70   **D.** 700

4. $900 \div$ ■ $= 300$

   A. 3   **C.** 100
   B. 30   **D.** 300

Add or subtract.

5. $\dfrac{8}{10} - \dfrac{3}{10} =$ _____

6. $\dfrac{1}{8} + \dfrac{4}{8} =$ _____

7. Bill has 4 different fish: a beta, a black guppy, a common guppy, and a neon tetra. His fish are named Bubbles, Goldilocks, Speckles, and Zoe. Bubbles and Zoe are not guppies. Speckles is a black guppy. Zoe is not a tetra. What kind of fish is Goldilocks?

	Beta	Black Guppy	Common Guppy	Neon Tetra
Bubbles				
Goldilocks				
Speckles				
Zoe				

_____

_____

Spiral Review and Test Prep 12-4

Circle the correct answer.

1. The tens digit of a three-digit number is 4. The ones digit is 1 greater than the tens digit and the tens digit is 1 greater than the hundreds digit. What is the number?

A. 146   **C.** 345
B. 247   **D.** 446

2. Rachel bought a 2 L container of vegetable oil. She has 1,250 mL left. How much vegetable oil has she used?

A. 250 mL
B. 500 mL
C. 750 mL
D. 1 L 750 mL

3. Use mental math to find 381 − 218.

A. 63   **C.** 163
B. 73   **D.** 173

Multiply.

4. $2.57 × 3 =

_____

5. $1.14 × 5 =

_____

6. Manny spent $4.50 on food and $6.00 on videos. He had $9.75 left. How much did he start with? Explain how you found your answer.

_____

_____

_____

_____

_____

_____

_____

_____

Name_____

Spiral Review and Test Prep 12-5

Circle the correct answer.

1. Which is the best estimate for 61 ÷ 7?

   A. 2   **C.** 5
   B. 3   **D.** 9

2. Which is the quotient of 84 ÷ 4?

   A. 15 R3   **C.** 20 R8
   B. 16   **D.** 21

3. Paul left school and walked for 10 min to the library. He spent 55 min at the library, then 25 min walking home with his friends. Paul arrived at home at 4:15 P.M. What time did Paul leave school?

   A. 2:45 P.M.
   B. 3:15 P.M.
   C. 3:35 P.M.
   D. 3:45 P.M.

4. Is 1 lb 7 oz more or less than 25 oz? Explain.

   _____

   _____

   _____

   _____

5. Ben, Jeff, and Sam play baseball, soccer, and tennis. They each play a different sport. Ben does not play baseball or soccer. Sam does not play baseball. What sport does Sam play?

   _____

6.

   What is the decimal for the shaded part?

   _____

© Pearson Education, Inc. 3

Spiral Review and Test Prep 12-6

Circle the correct answer.

1. A box has 37 paper clips in it. Each project needs 5 paper clips. About how many projects can be completed with the box of paper clips?

   A. About 5
   B. About 7
   C. About 9
   D. About 11

2. Which is the best estimate for the mass of a cat?

   A. 5 g   **C.** 5 kg
   B. 50 g   **D.** 500 kg

3. How many pounds and ounces is a 24 oz box of cereal?

   A. 1 lb 4 oz
   B. 1 lb 8 oz
   C. 2 lb
   D. 2 lb 4 oz

4. Which is greater, 51 ÷ 9 or 51 ÷ 7? How do you know?

   _____

   _____

   _____

5. Groups of geese, nightingales, peacocks, and pheasants are called either a muster, a nide, a skein, or a watch. A group of geese is not called a muster or a watch. A group of nightingales is not called a muster. Complete the table to find what each group of birds is called.

	Muster	Nide	Skein	Watch
Geese		No		
Nightingales		No		
Peacocks		No		
Pheasants	No	Yes	No	No

Spiral Review and Test Prep 12-7

Circle the correct answer.

1. Which is the best estimate for the product of 5 × 58?

   A. 200   **C.** 400

   B. 300   **D.** 450

2. Which is the product of 73 × 4?

   A. 280   **C.** 292

   B. 282   **D.** 300

3. At which temperature would you be most likely to water ski?

   A. 30°C   **C.** 50°C

   B. 30°F   **D.** 50°F

4. Four friends are standing in a straight line. In how many different ways can they be arranged?

   A. 4   **C.** 18

   B. 8   **D.** 24

5. Find the next two numbers in the pattern and describe the pattern.

5, 8, 11, _____, _____

_____

6. Explain how to find the number of grams in 3 kg.

_____

_____

_____

7. A four-digit number uses only two different digits. The number in the ones, tens, and thousands place is the same. The number in the hundreds place is double the number in the ones place. The ones place digit plus the tens place digit is 6. What is the number?

_____

Spiral Review and Test Prep 12-8

Circle the correct answer.

1. Which is the best description for 70°F?

   A. Burning   **C.** Cool
   B. Warm   **D.** Cold

2. Jeremy is a high school student. Describe the chances that Jeremy will attend school today.

   A. Certain
   B. Likely
   C. Unlikely
   D. Impossible

3. Use mental math to find the quotient of 48 ÷ 2.

   A. 12   **C.** 21
   B. 14   **D.** 24

4. Which is the quotient of 210 ÷ 7?

   A. 3   **C.** 300
   B. 30   **D.** 3,000

The table shows the number of people from Northern states who signed the Declaration of Independence.

State	Signers
Connecticut	4
Delaware	3
Massachusetts	5
New Hampshire	3
New Jersey	5
New York	4
TOTAL	24

5. Write the fraction of signers who were from Delaware.

_____

6. A group of 44 students is going on a ride. Each seat on the ride holds 3 students. How many seats will the group need?

_____

Spiral Review and Test Prep 12-9

Circle the correct answer.

1. What is the chance of spinning a 3?

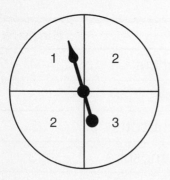

   A. 1 out of 3
   B. 1 out of 4
   C. 2 out of 3
   D. 2 out of 4

2. The numbers 1–6 are on a cube. Describe the event of tossing a 5.

   A. Certain
   B. Likely
   C. Unlikely
   D. Impossible

3.

What is the volume of the cube? Give your answer in cubic units.

_____

Multiply.

4. $807 \times 6 =$ _____

5. $415 \times 5 =$ _____

6. Mr. Brown, Mrs. Frodo, and Mr. Wilson have an iguana, a hamster, and a mouse in their classrooms. Mrs. Frodo's class has a mouse. Mr. Brown's class does not have the hamster. What pet does Mr. Wilson's class have?

_____

Spiral Review and Test Prep 12-10

Circle the correct answer.

1. There are 19 people going on a camping trip. Each van will hold 4 people and their camping gear. How many vans are needed?

A. 3 C. 5
B. 4 D. 6

2. Which is the product of 7 × 27?

A. 149 C. 189
B. 156 D. 197

3. Which comes next in the pattern?

12, 16, 20, ▨

A. 22 C. 24
B. 23 D. 25

4. Find the product of 33 × 9.

A. 297 C. 281
B. 288 D. 272

5.

What is the probability of drawing a card that is less than 5?

_____

6.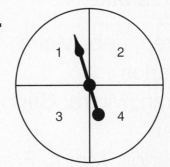

What is the chance of spinning a number greater than 2?

_____

Spiral Review and Test Prep 12-11

Circle the correct answer.

1. Moira, Jeb, Carlos, and Fran each had their picture taken. Fran went first, and Jeb went last. Moira had her picture taken before Carlos. In which order did the students have their pictures taken?

   A. Fran, Jeb, Moira, Carlos

   B. Fran, Moira, Carlos, Jeb

   C. Carlos, Moira, Fran, Jeb

   D. Fran, Carlos, Moira, Jeb

2. Round 454 to the nearest hundred.

   A. 400   C. 455

   B. 450   D. 500

3. What is the probability of spinning red?

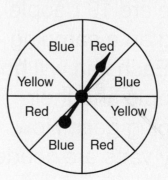

_____

Divide.

4. $87 \div 4 =$ _____

5. $41 \div 3 =$ _____

6. Explain how you can find the number of ounces in 4 lb.